Mark Marchesi

EVANGELINE

A Modern Tale of Acadia

Daylight

Cofounders: Taj Forer and Michael Itkoff
Creative Director: Ursula Damm
Copy editor: Elissa Rabellino
Editorial Assistant: Dasha Kabanova

ISBN 978-1-942084-21-1

Printed in China

Daylight Books
E-mail: info@daylightbooks.org
Web: www.daylightbooks.org

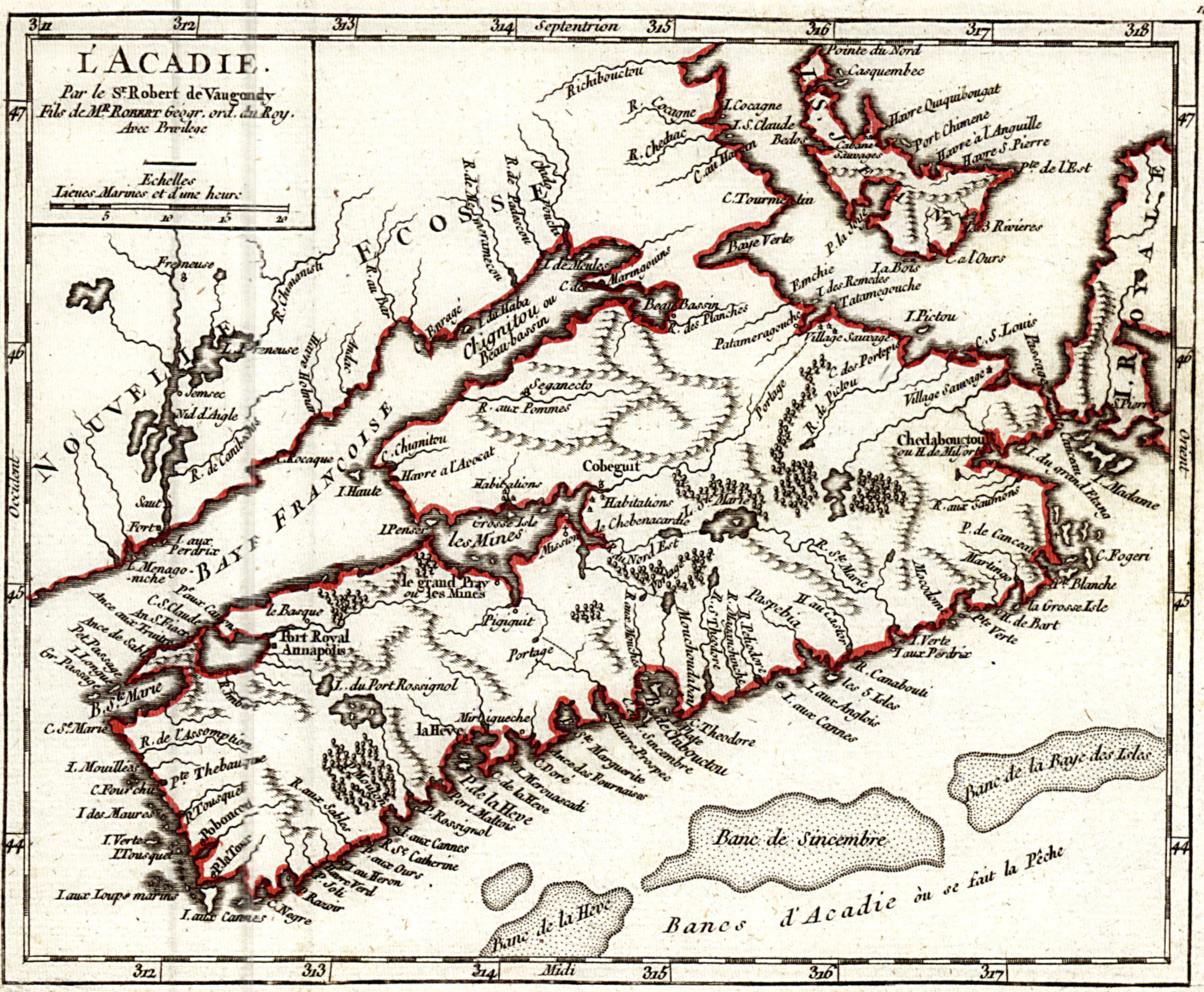
L'ACADIE.
Par le Sr. Robert de Vaugondy
Fils de Mr. Robert Geogr. ord. du Roy.
Avec Privilege
Echelles
Lieues Marines et d'une heure
5 10 15 20
Septentrion
Midi
Occident
Orient
NOUVELLE ECOSSE
BAYE FRANCOISE
Chignitou ou Beau-bassin
Port Royal
Annapolis
les Mines
le grand Pray ou les Mines
Cobeguit
Chedabouctou ou H. de Milfort
Banc de Sincembre
Banc de la Heve
Banc de la Baye des Isles
Bancs d'Acadie où se fait la Pêche
Baye Verte
C. Tourmentin
Pointe du Nord
Casquembec
Havre Quiquibougat
Port Chimene
Havre à l'Anguille
Havre S. Pierre
Pte. de l'Est
3 Rivieres
C. a l'Ours
I. Pictou
C. S. Louis
Tatamegouche
Village Sauvage
Richibouctou
R. Cocagne
I. Cocagne
I. S. Claude
R. Chediac
Bedos
I. de Meules
Maringouins
Beau Bassin
R. des Planches
Patameragouche
Seganecto
R. aux Pommes
C. Chignitou
Havre a l'Avocat
I. Haute
Habitations
Grosse Isle
I. Penser
Mission
le Chebenacardie
R. du Nord Est
Pigiquit
Portage
I. du Port Rossignol
la Heve
Mirliguesche
P. de la Heve
Port Maltois
P. Rossignol
I. aux Cannes
R. Ste. Catherine
I. aux Ours
I. au Heron
Havre Verd
P. Joli
I. Razoir
C. Negre
I. aux Cannes
I. aux Loups marins
I. Tousquet
I. Verte
I. des Maures
C. Fourchu
I. Mouillés
C. Ste. Marie
B. Ste. Marie
R. de l'Assomption
Pte. Thebauque
R. Tousquet
Pobomcoup
R. aux Sables
Freneuse
L. Freneuse
Jemsec
Nid d'Aigle
R. de Canibas
Saut
Fort
I. aux Perdrix
I. Menago-niche
C. Rocaque
le Basque
C. S. Claude
Ance de Sable
I. Longue
Gr. Passage
Pet. Passage
I. Ste. Marie
Mouchoudabou
R. S. Theodore
R. Pelecdore
I. Verte
I. aux Perdrix
R. Canabouti
les 5 Isles
I. aux Anglois
I. aux Cannes
C. Theodore
B. de Chibouctou
Sincembre
Havre Prospec
Ste. Marguerite
Ance des Fournaises
C. Doré
I. Merouascadi
Ile de la Heve
R. Ste. Marie
Havre au Castor
Paspebia
Musquodobo
Martingo
C. Fogeri
Pte. Blanche
la Grosse Isle
H. de Bart
Pte. Verte
P. de Canceau
R. aux Saumons
I. Madame
I. du grand Etang
Canceau
S. Pierre
Village Sauvage
C. des Portepi
R. de Pictou
I. la Bois
P. la Joie
I. des Remedes
I. Chedabouctou
C. au Heron
Cabane Sauvages
I. R. ROYALE
47
46
45
44
311
312
313
314
315
316
317
318

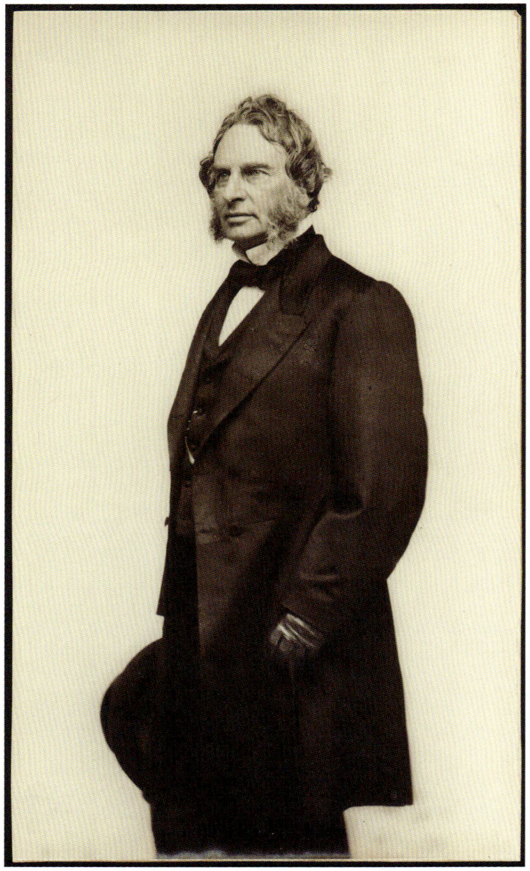

Preface

by Christoph Irmscher

Henry Wadsworth Longfellow's *Evangeline: A Tale of Acadie* (1847), one of the most popular poems in the history of American literature, began its life not in the "forest primeval" it so skillfully evokes but at the dinner table in Longfellow's stately house on Brattle Street in Cambridge, Massachusetts. Nathaniel Hawthorne, Longfellow's former classmate from Bowdoin, had come for a visit, and he brought with him a friend, the Reverend Horace Conolly. Conolly for quite a while had been trying to get Hawthorne interested in a story that one of his parishioners had shared with him: a heart-wrenching tale about the expulsion of thousands of Acadians from their homeland and, more particularly, about the desperate efforts of a young Acadian woman to be reunited with her lover. When Longfellow heard the story that night, he was immediately captivated. It was, he said, "the best illustration of the faithfulness and constancy of woman that I have ever heard or read." If he did not want the incident for one of his tales, Longfellow said to Hawthorne, "let me at least have it for a poem." Hawthorne agreed, and a few years later *Evangeline* was published, to great acclaim.

"Beautiful thoughts spring up like roses," exulted Hawthorne in his review for the *Salem Advertiser*. Longfellow's own assessment was more modest. "I hope Mr. Conolly does not think I spoilt the tale he told," he wrote to Hawthorne and thanked him once again for "resigning" the material to him: "This success I owe entirely to you, for being willing to forgo the pleasure of writing a prose tale, which many people would have taken for poetry, that I might write a poem which many people take for prose." I like the fact that the making of Longfellow's greatest poem was surrounded by acts of generosity and gratitude—and that Longfellow never forgot that he was merely the story's caretaker. A few weeks after his poem was published, Longfellow ventured into town, kids in tow, to buy some hats for them. As he got ready to pay for his purchases, the clerk beamed at him: "You will get part of this money back tomorrow for one of your books, Mr. Longfellow!"

The generous circulating and sharing of goods—of work and pleasure; of food, drink, songs, and tales—are the hallmarks of Acadian culture as Longfellow paints it in the first few pages of his poem. Our eyes travel over their vast meadows, lush orchards, and fertile fields of flax, their barns bursting with hay, the numberless flocks on their pastures. Good fences make good neighbors, we like to say, but that is not how Longfellow tells us the Acadians lived—their doors had no locks, their windows no bars, and their dwellings were as open as their hearts: "There the richest was poor, and the poorest lived in abundance."

At night, resting from the labors of the day, the Acadians would assemble by their fireplaces and sing ancient songs while the spinning wheels clacked and the clocks ticked. Or they would listen to the tales told by Rene Leblanc, the wizened village notary, about the *loup-garou* ("werewolf") in the forest, of goblins that brought the horses water at night, or of ghosts of unbaptized children that haunted their dreams. They would hear how the oxen suddenly started talking on Christmas Eve and how a spider shut up in a nutshell would cure a fever.

But the story that trumped all others was the one about the orphan girl who, long ago in the old country, was suspected of having stolen a pearl necklace from a nobleman's palace and was burned to death. As her spirit ascended, the bronze statue of justice in the town square shattered and the scales it held in its left hand clattered to the ground, revealing, in the cracks of the pavement, the nest of a magpie and, in the nest's lining, the missing necklace. The stories told and listened to by the Acadians—stories that spoke of fear and suffering but also of miracles and healing and justice finally rendered (though too little and too late)—reflect in miniature the tale that Longfellow himself wanted to tell with his poem: a tale about loss and the hope for a recovery, however faint, insufficient, imperfect.

To be sure, the losses that Longfellow's poem records are tremendous. The French-speaking Acadians had settled in the course of the 17th century on the eastern coast of Canada, eventually becoming pawns in the endless power struggle over that territory between the French and the English. Their expulsion—ordered by the British in 1755—turned farmers and craftsmen who had become solidly rooted in their environment into instant refugees. The "*grand dérangement*," as it is appropriately known, was a brutal event that has assumed mythical dimensions in the collective memory of French Canada. Families were broken up and scattered. Longfellow's poem describes the expulsion as what it was: a genocide that left the shores of the bay littered with the bodies of the dead. Who could forget the horrifying image of the fire consuming the village of Grand-Pré as a dark moon rose over its roofs and flames burst through the thick sheets of smoke "like the quivering hands of a martyr"?

While some Acadians—represented by Basil the Blacksmith in Longfellow's poem—eventually settled in Louisiana, others continued to wander across the continent. Evangeline, searching for traces of her lover, Gabriel, from the swamps of the South to the prairies of the West to the cities of the East, where the only reminders of trees are the streets named after them, became the patron saint for exiles all over the world, a symbol for the terrible price that enforced displacement exacts to this day from migrants anywhere. At the foot of the Ozarks, a Shawnee woman enters Evangeline's makeshift camp and tells her about her lost—indeed, murdered—lover, and the stories and tears both women share are among the most intensely egalitarian moments in all of American literature.

Longfellow had never seen Acadia, just as he had not been to the Ozarks or to Louisiana, with its "sluggish waters" and trees festooned with Spanish moss that he so memorably evokes in the second part of the poem. But the mind of this most cosmopolitan of American poets went wherever it wanted to go. In a bitterly ironic twist, he chose to end his poem in Philadelphia, the City of Brotherly Love, where Evangeline and Gabriel finally meet again, although too late to enjoy their union. But, as the pacific and incorrigibly optimistic Longfellow would argue, even justice that comes too late is worth the wait. The dead bodies of Evangeline and Gabriel resting in their graves in the little Catholic cemetery at the heart of Quaker City are a reminder to all of us that the best and most authentic stories we share aren't the easier ones.

In *Evangeline*, Longfellow wanted to write an American epic, and he succeeded. Classical hexameters don't work well in English, but to Longfellow occasional clumsiness seemed a risk worth taking. Forget about the details—the lines that may sound contrived and awkward today—and think, instead, about the challenge that the poem must have posed to the reading sensibilities of the American public in 1847: an English poem written in classical meter about the displacement of a Francophone community, featuring not a male protagonist (Gabriel might be one of the dullest characters in the history of the epic) but a powerfully determined woman whose resolve never weakens even as she is aging before our eyes.

Longfellow's poem ends as it began, mournfully, as the murmuring forest laments the absence of those who, in better days, dwelled in its leafy shadows. The thatched-roofed comfort of the Acadians has long yielded to another culture, "with other customs and language." But some Acadians are still there, carrying on with their lives, and now—and here Longfellow self-consciously envisions his poem's afterlife—the stories they tell each other also include, as indeed they do to this day, the one about the resilient Evangeline.

Longfellow could not have anticipated his poem's popularity with modern Acadians, and he would have been surprised by the role it would play in the emergence of Acadian nationalism. But the canny businessman in him would have been pleased that the descendants of the formerly deported named one of their newspapers after him. And the poet, whose influence, as an African American newspaper put it after his death, "was always given on the side of liberty," would have been even happier to see that his poem has helped keep alive the memory of a historic injustice done to a peaceful people. For example, *Evangeline* directly inspired "Acadian Driftwood," a popular song composed in 1975 by Robbie Robertson of the Band. Its last lines, sung in French, express the same mixture of longing and deprivation that Longfellow captured so well in his poem:

> *Sais tu, Acadie, j'ai le mal du pays*
> *Ta neige, Acadie, fait des larmes au soleil*
> (You know, Acadia, I am homesick for you
> Your snow, Acadia, makes tears in the sun)

That same sense of pain has more recently pervaded the poignant photographs of modern Acadia taken by Mark Marchesi, an unforgettable, brilliant tribute to the persistence of Longfellow's vision even in our century. Loss and loneliness have written themselves into the crumbling paint, shattered windows, and broken roofs of abandoned houses; into the docked fishing boats and empty churches, the mist-shrouded bays and darkening clouds that Marchesi's camera has captured. The sun is setting over these landscapes emptied of human presence, painting them pink with soft despair—a quiet reminder that words alone cannot undo the terrible damage wrought by history. And yet, on another level, Marchesi's work too becomes a part—an important and hopeful one—of a continuing, vibrant tradition of stories woven around a landscape that the poet Longfellow, more than 150 years ago, imagined as forever filled with a dreamy and magical light.

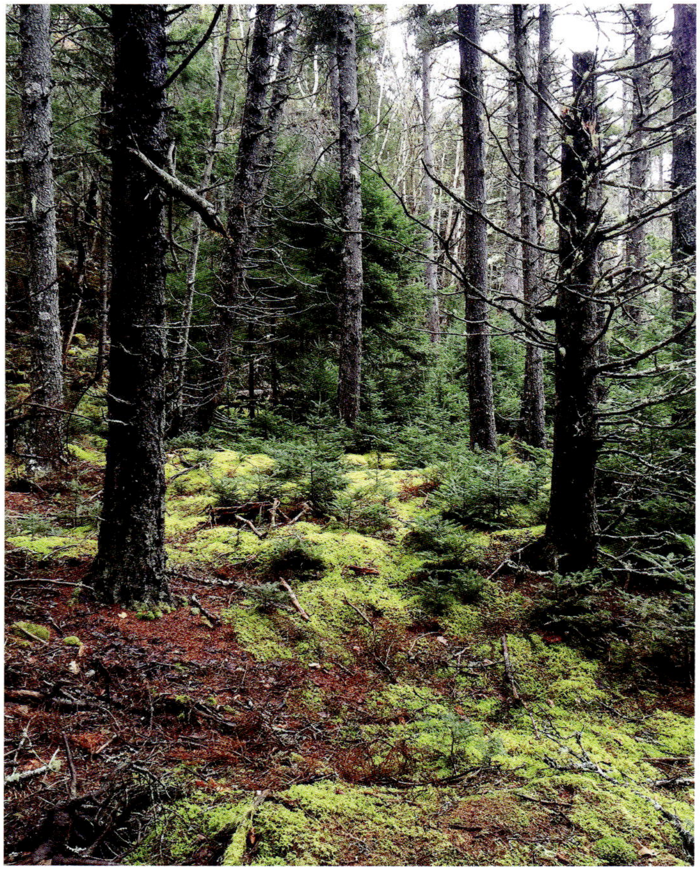

Selection

from H.W. Longfellow's Evangeline

This is the forest primeval. The murmuring pines and the hemlocks,
Bearded with moss, and in garments green, indistinct in the twilight,
Stand like Druids of eld, with voices sad and prophetic,
Stand like harpers hoar, with beards that rest on their bosoms.
Loud from its rocky caverns, the deep-voiced neighboring ocean
Speaks, and in accents disconsolate answers the wail of the forest.

This is the forest primeval; but where are the hearts that beneath it
Leaped like the roe, when he hears in the woodland the voice of the huntsman?
Where is the thatch-roofed village, the home of Acadian farmers,—
Men whose lives glided on like rivers that water the woodlands,
Darkened by shadows of earth, but reflecting an image of heaven?
Waste are those pleasant farms, and the farmers forever departed!
Scattered like dust and leaves, when the mighty blasts of October
Seize them, and whirl them aloft, and sprinkle them far o'er the ocean
Naught but tradition remains of the beautiful village of Grand-Pré.

Ye who believe in affection that hopes, and endures, and is patient,
Ye who believe in the beauty and strength of woman's devotion,
List to the mournful tradition, still sung by the pines of the forest;
List to a Tale of Love in Acadie, home of the happy.

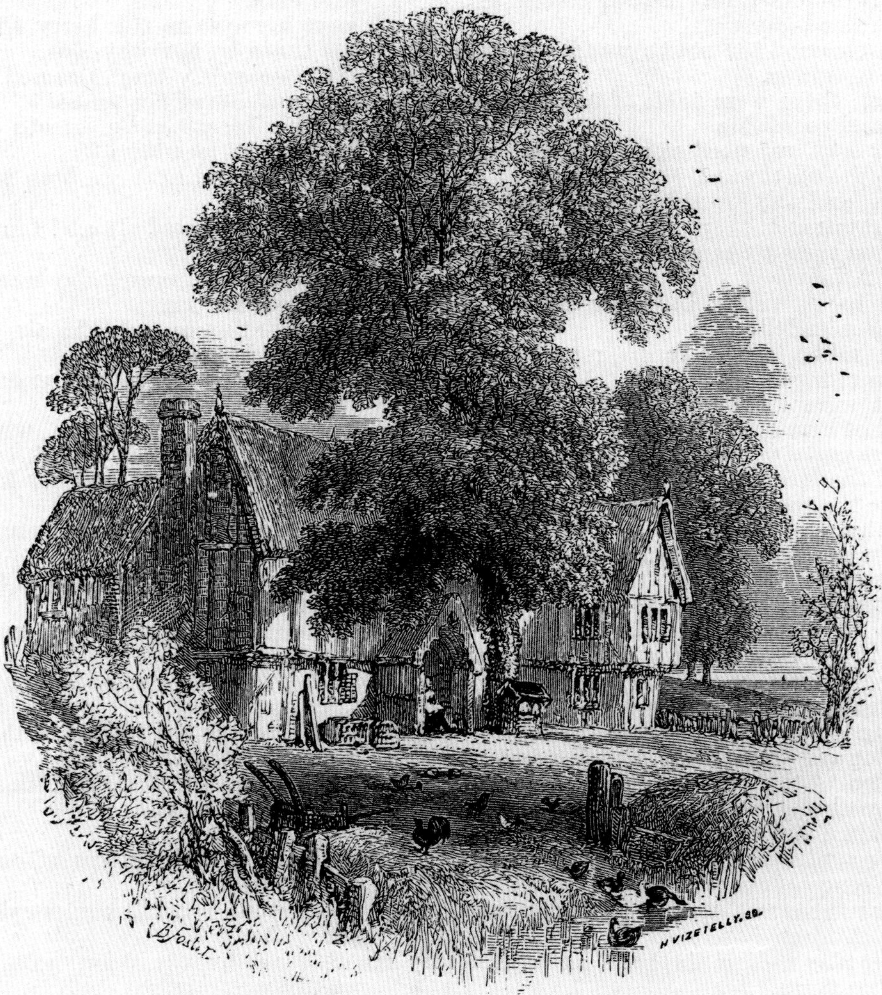

Firmly builded with rafters of oak, the house of the farmer.

In the Acadian land, on the shores of the Basin of Minas,
Distant, secluded, still, the little village of Grand-Pré
Lay in the fruitful valley. Vast meadows stretched to the eastward,
Giving the village its name, and pasture to flocks without number.
Dikes, that the hands of the farmers had raised with labor incessant,
Shut out the turbulent tides; but at stated seasons the flood-gates
Opened, and welcomed the sea to wander at will o'er the meadows.
West and south there were fields of flax, and orchards and cornfields
Spreading afar and unfenced o'er the plain; and away to the northward
Blomidon rose, and the forests old, and aloft on the mountains
Sea-fogs pitched their tents, and mists from the mighty Atlantic
Looked on the happy valley, but ne'er from their station descended.
There, in the midst of its farms, reposed the Acadian village.
Strongly built were the houses, with frames of oak and of hemlock,
Such as the peasants of Normandy built in the reign of the Henries.
Thatched were the roofs, with dormer-windows; and gables projecting
Over the basement below protected and shaded the doorway.

There in the tranquil evenings of summer, when brightly the sunset
Lighted the village street, and gilded the vanes on the chimneys,
Matrons and maidens sat in snow-white caps and in kirtles
Scarlet and blue and green, with distaffs spinning the golden
Flax for the gossiping looms, whose noisy shuttles within doors
Mingled their sounds with the whir of the wheels and the songs of the maidens.
Solemnly down the street came the parish priest, and the children
Paused in their play to kiss the hand he extended to bless them.
Reverend walked he among them; and up rose matrons and maidens,
Hailing his slow approach with words of affectionate welcome.
Then came the laborers home from the field, and serenely the sun sank
Down to his rest, and twilight prevailed. Anon from the belfry
Softly the Angelus sounded, and over the roofs of the village
Columns of pale blue smoke, like clouds of incense ascending,
Rose from a hundred hearths, the homes of peace and contentment.

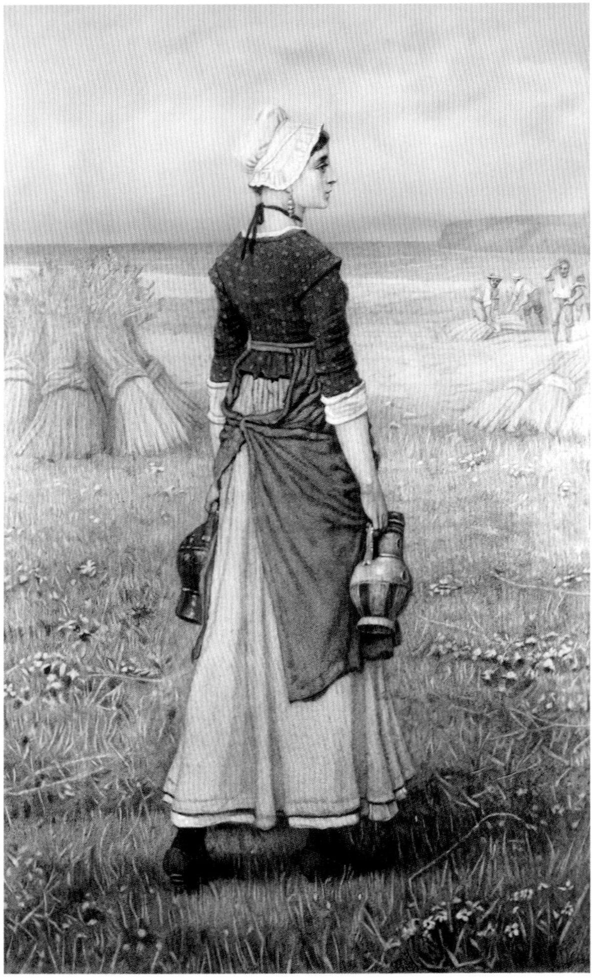

Thus dwelt together in love these simple Acadian farmers,—
Dwelt in the love of God and of man. Alike were they free from
Fear, that reigns with the tyrant, and envy, the vice of republics.
Neither locks had they to their doors, nor bars to their windows;
But their dwellings were open as day and the hearts of the owners;
There the richest was poor, and the poorest lived in abundance.

Somewhat apart from the village, and nearer the Basin of Minas,
Benedict Bellefontaine, the wealthiest farmer of Grand-Pré,
Dwelt on his goodly acres; and with him, directing his household,
Gentle Evangeline lived, his child, and the pride of the village.
Stalwart and stately in form was the man of seventy winters;
Hearty and hale was he, an oak that is covered with snowflakes;
White as the snow were his locks, and his cheeks as brown as the oak-leaves.
Fair was she to behold, that maiden of seventeen summers.
Black were her eyes as the berry that grows on the thorn by the wayside,
Black, yet how softly they gleamed beneath the brown shade of her tresses!
Sweet was her breath as the breath of kine that feed in the meadows.
When in the harvest heat she bore to the reapers at noontide
Flagons of home-brewed ale, ah! fair in sooth was the maiden.

Fairer was she when, on Sunday morn, while the bell from its turret
Sprinkled with holy sounds the air, as the priest with his hyssop
Sprinkles the congregation, and scatters blessings upon them,
Down the long street she passed, with her chaplet of beads and her missal,
Wearing her Norman cap, and her kirtle of blue, and the ear-rings,
Brought in the olden time from France, and since, as an heirloom,
Handed down from mother to child, through long generations.
But a celestial brightness—a more ethereal beauty—
Shone on her face and encircled her form, when, after confession,
Homeward serenely she walked with God's benediction upon her.
When she had passed, it seemed like the ceasing of exquisite music.

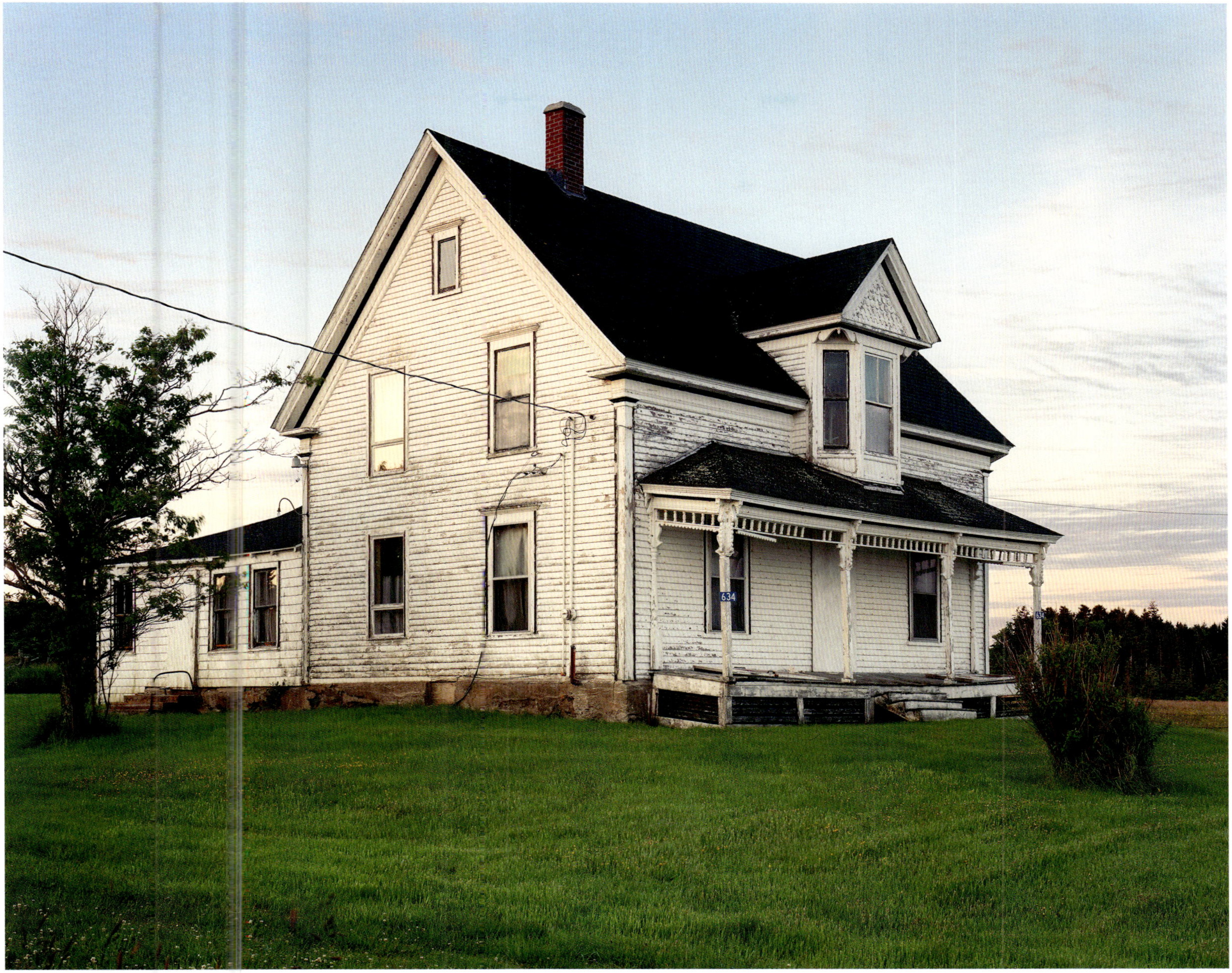

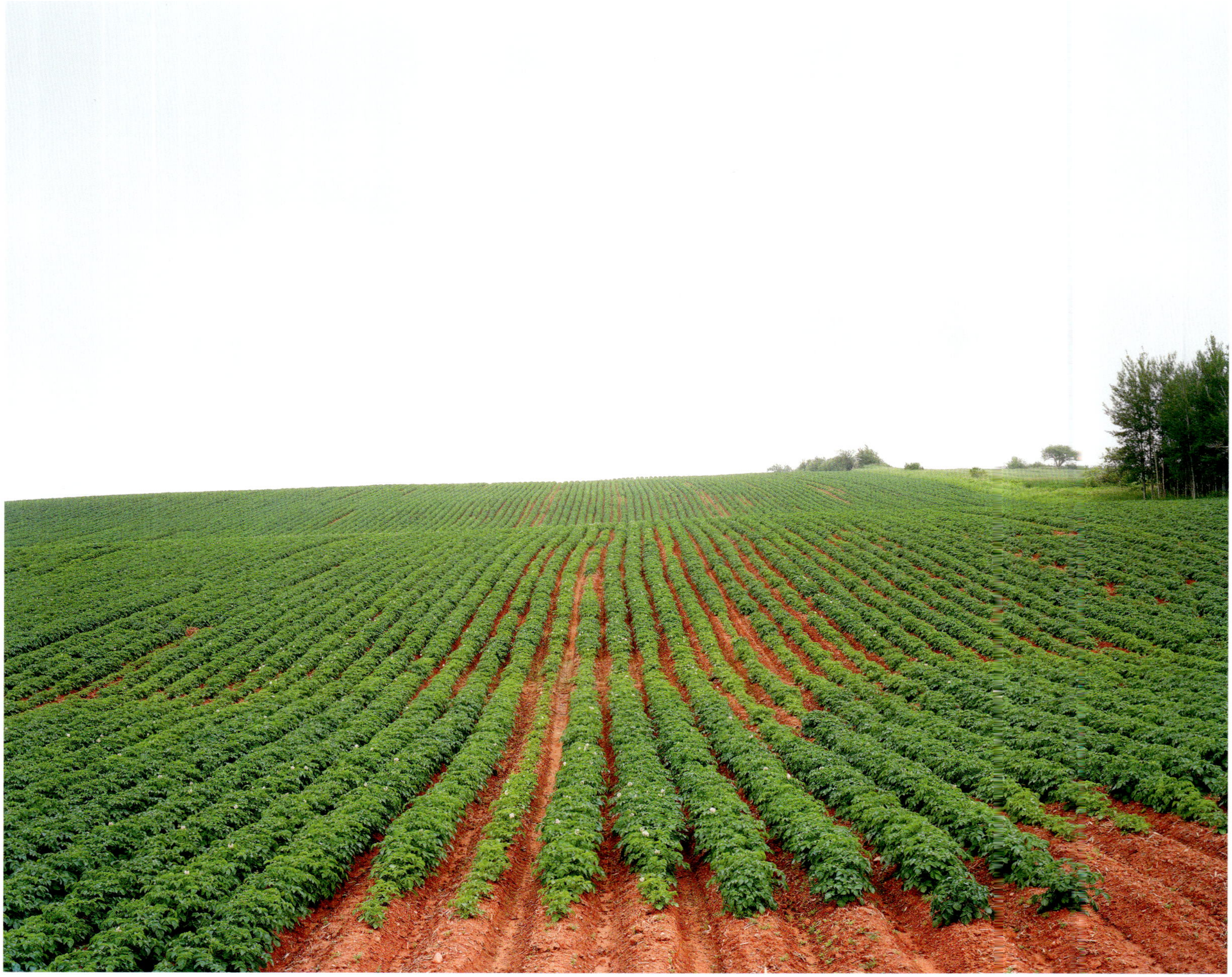

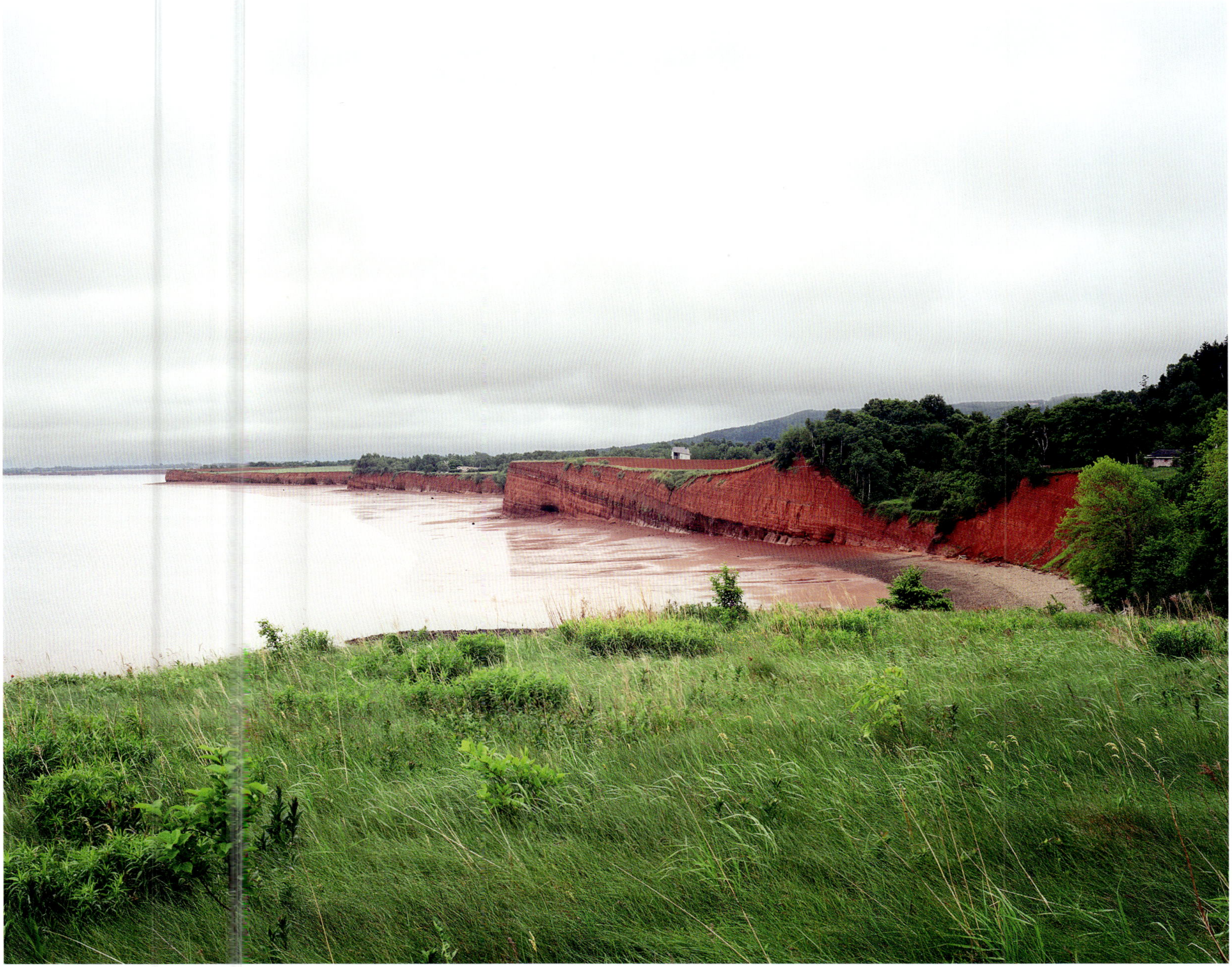

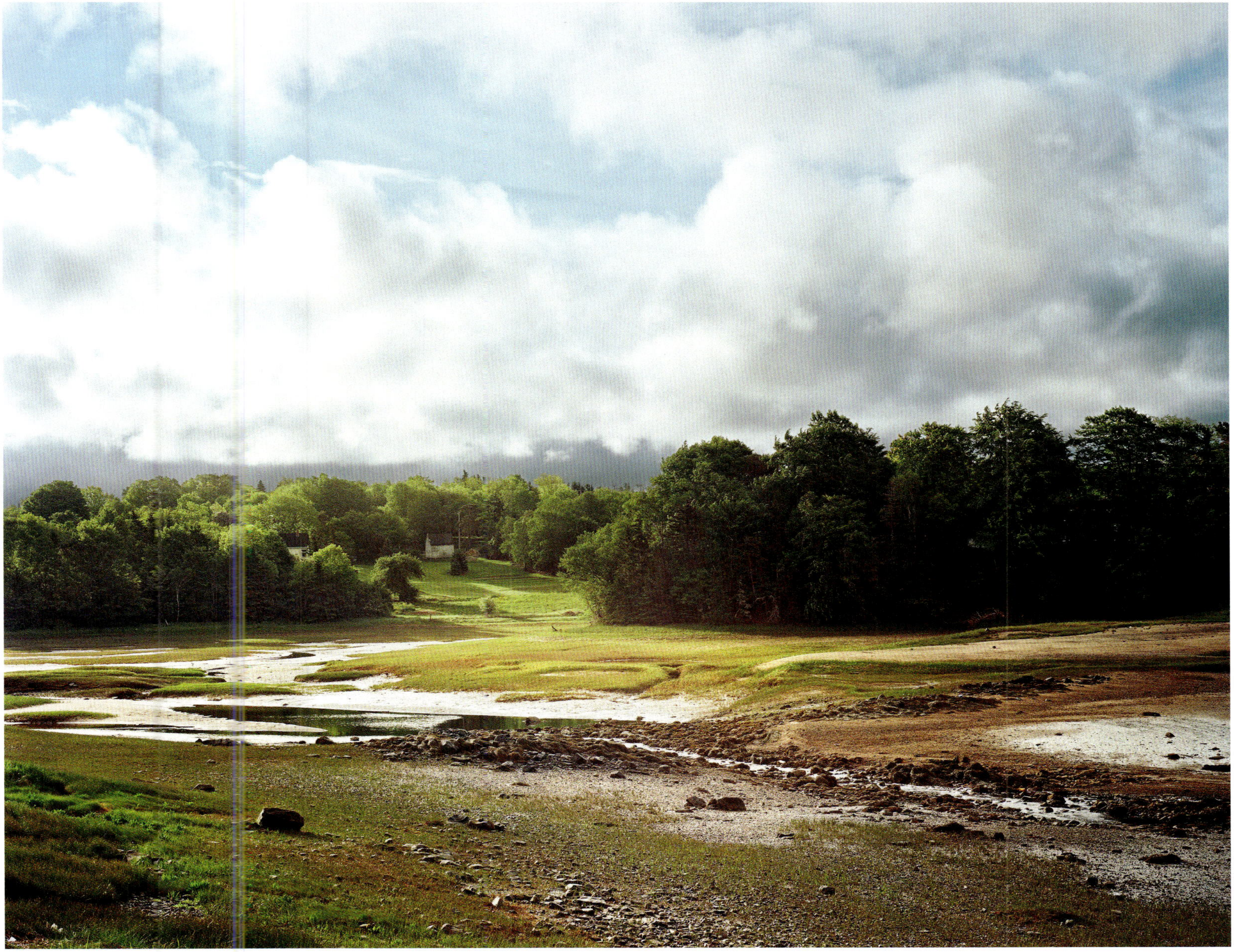

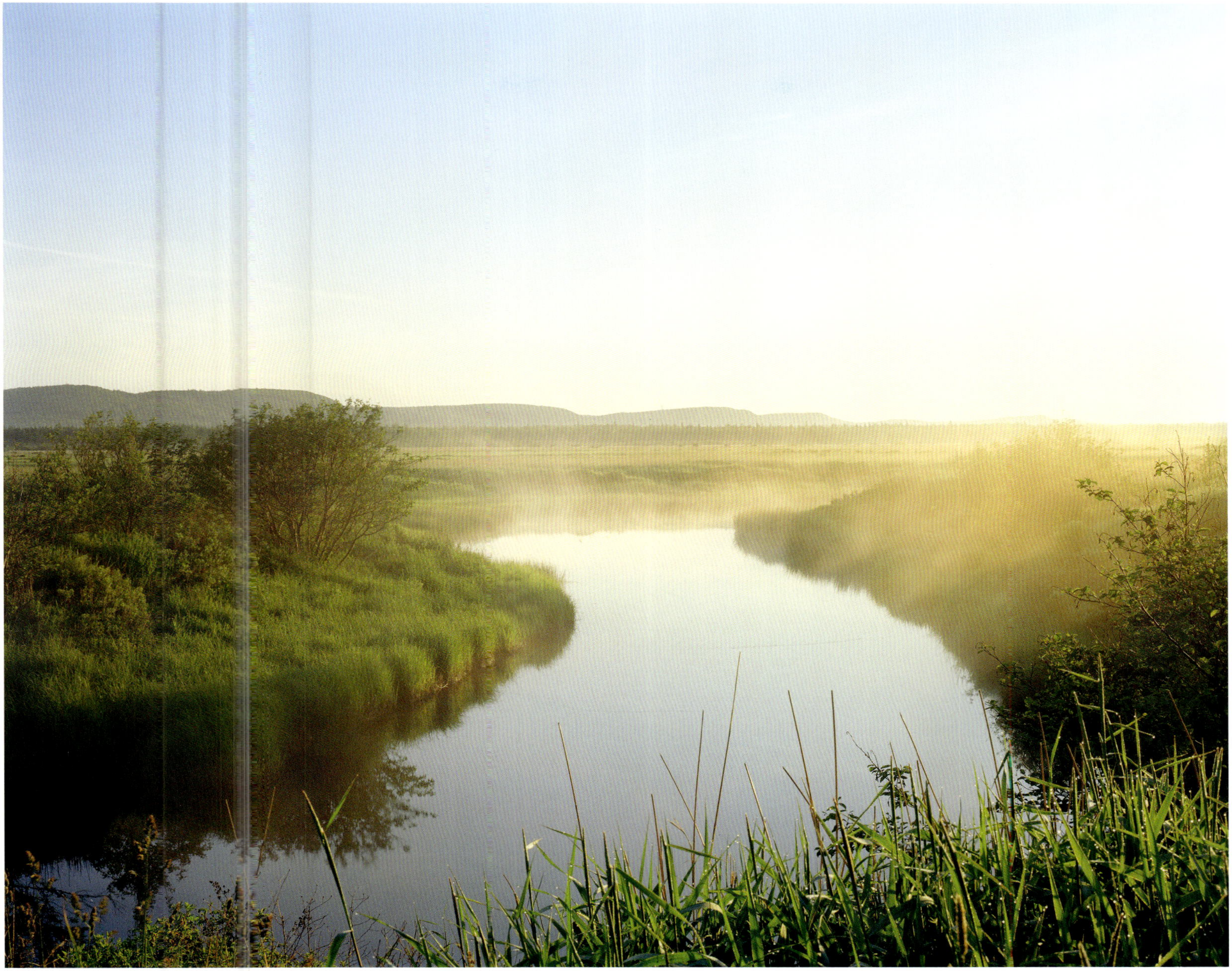

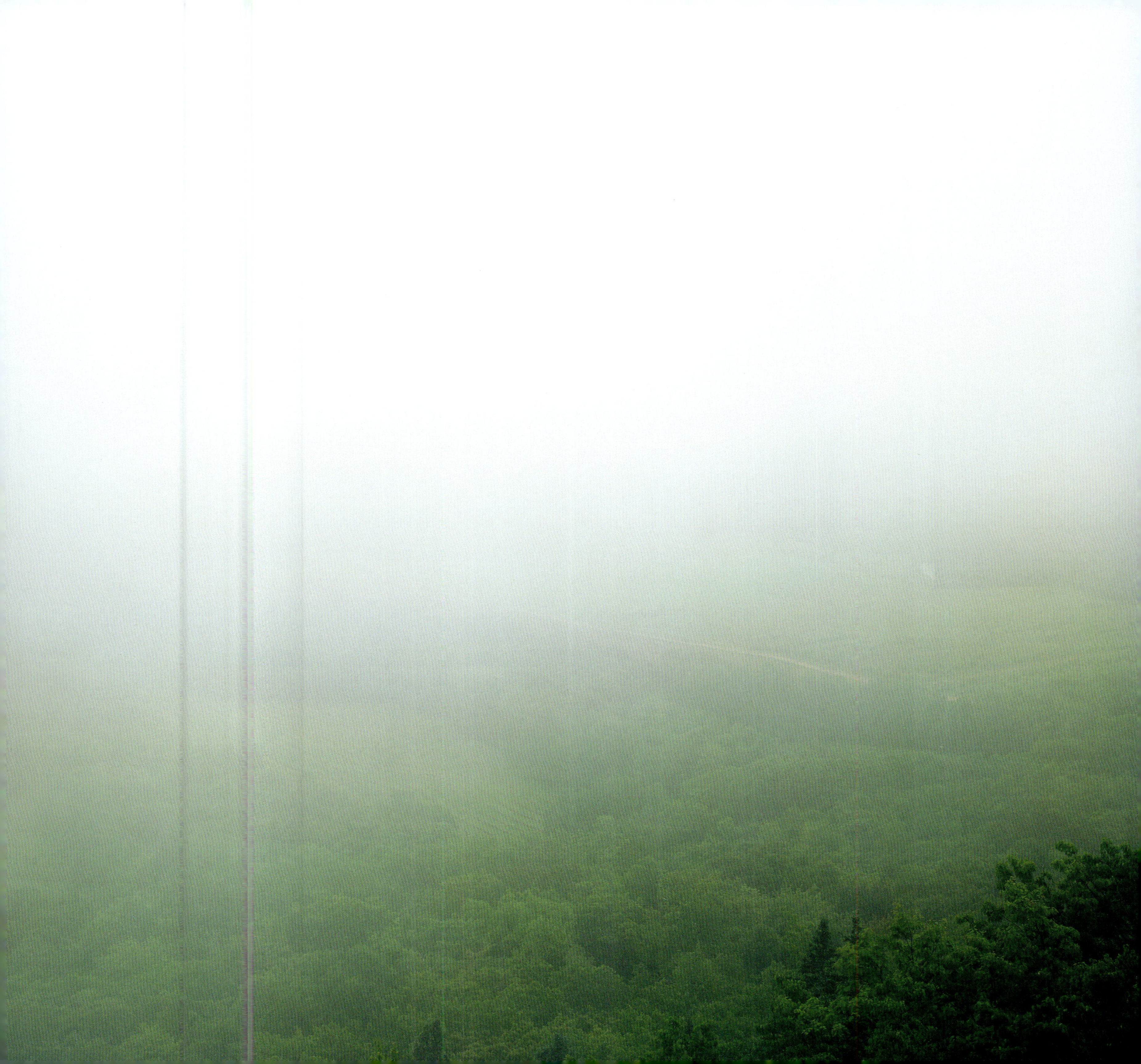

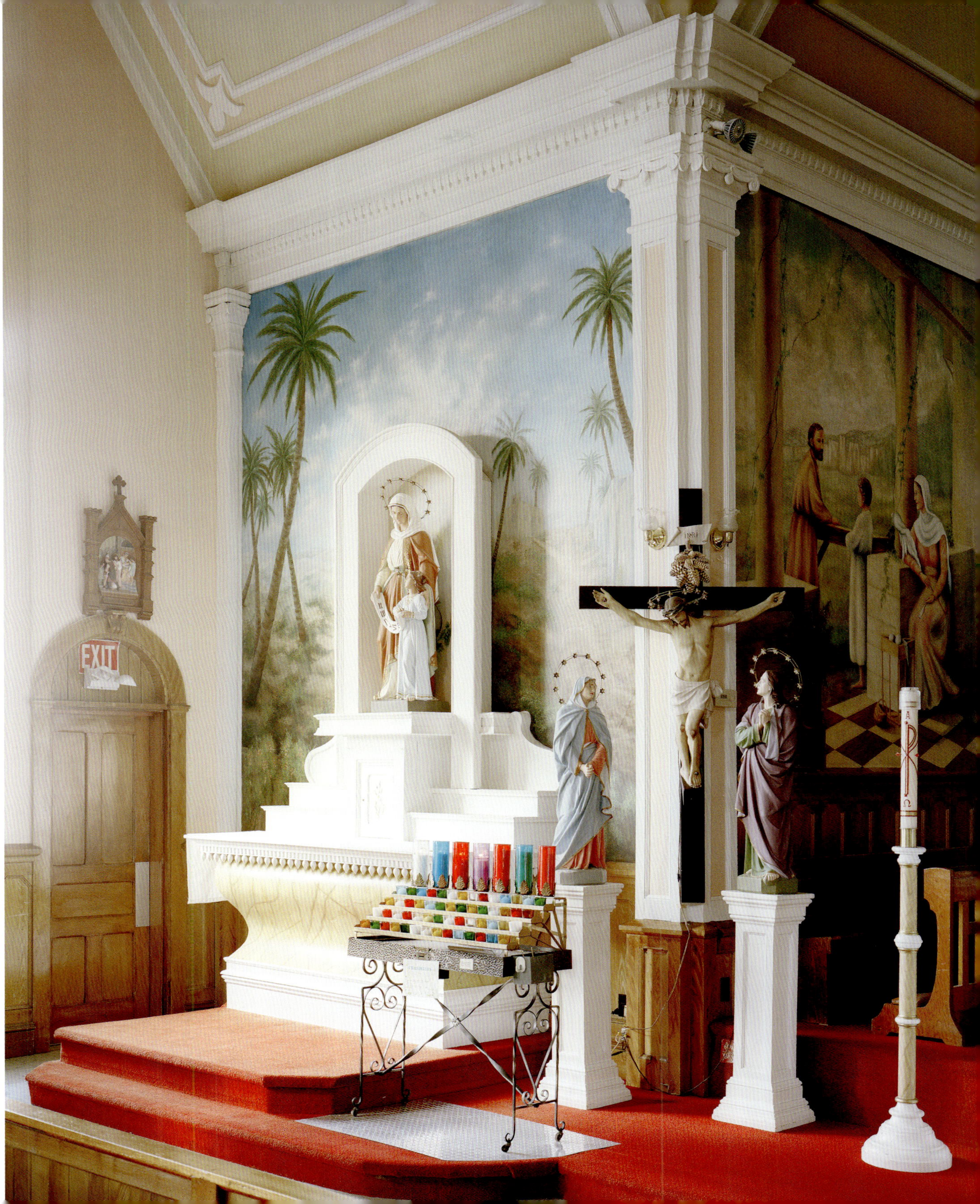
EXIT

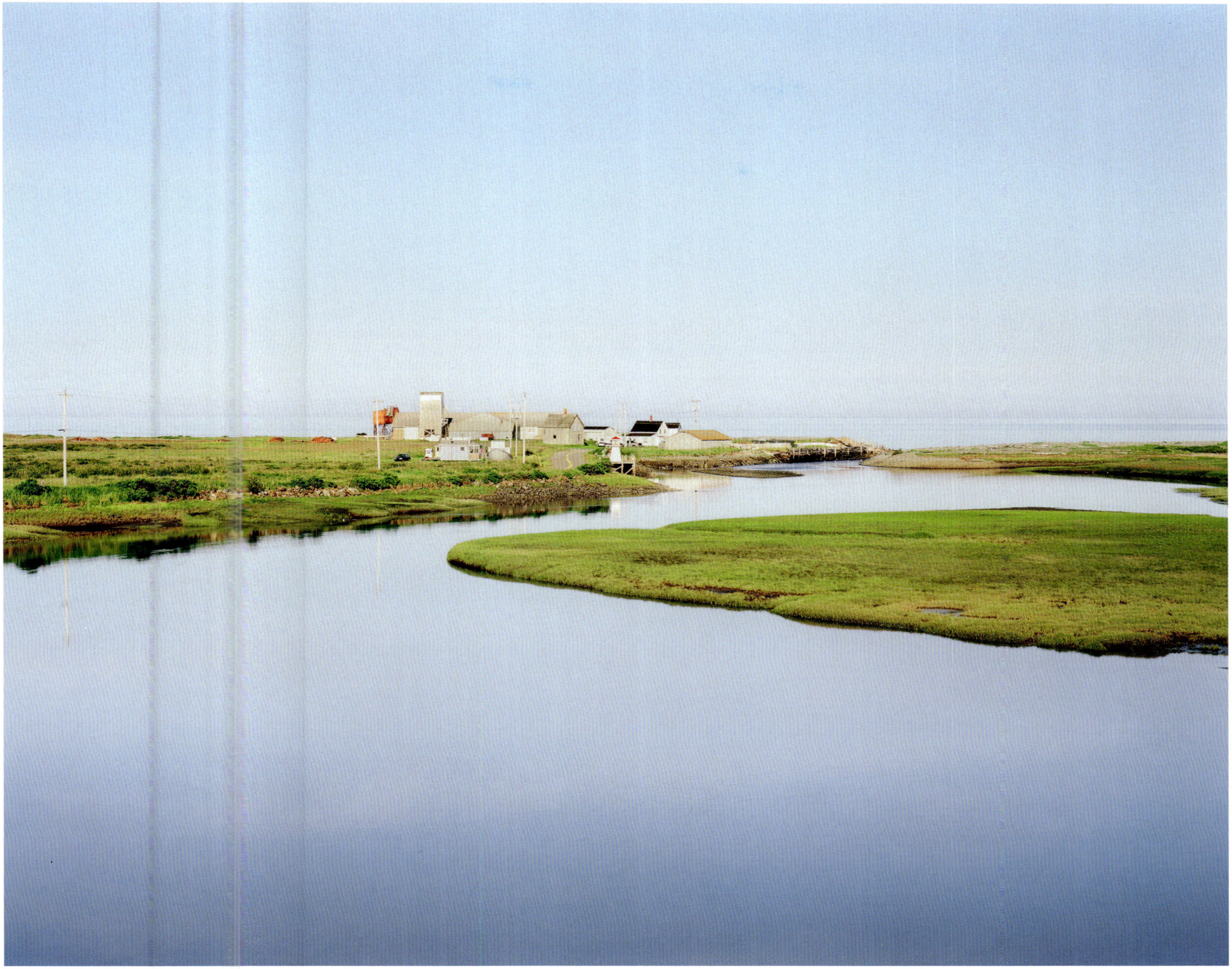

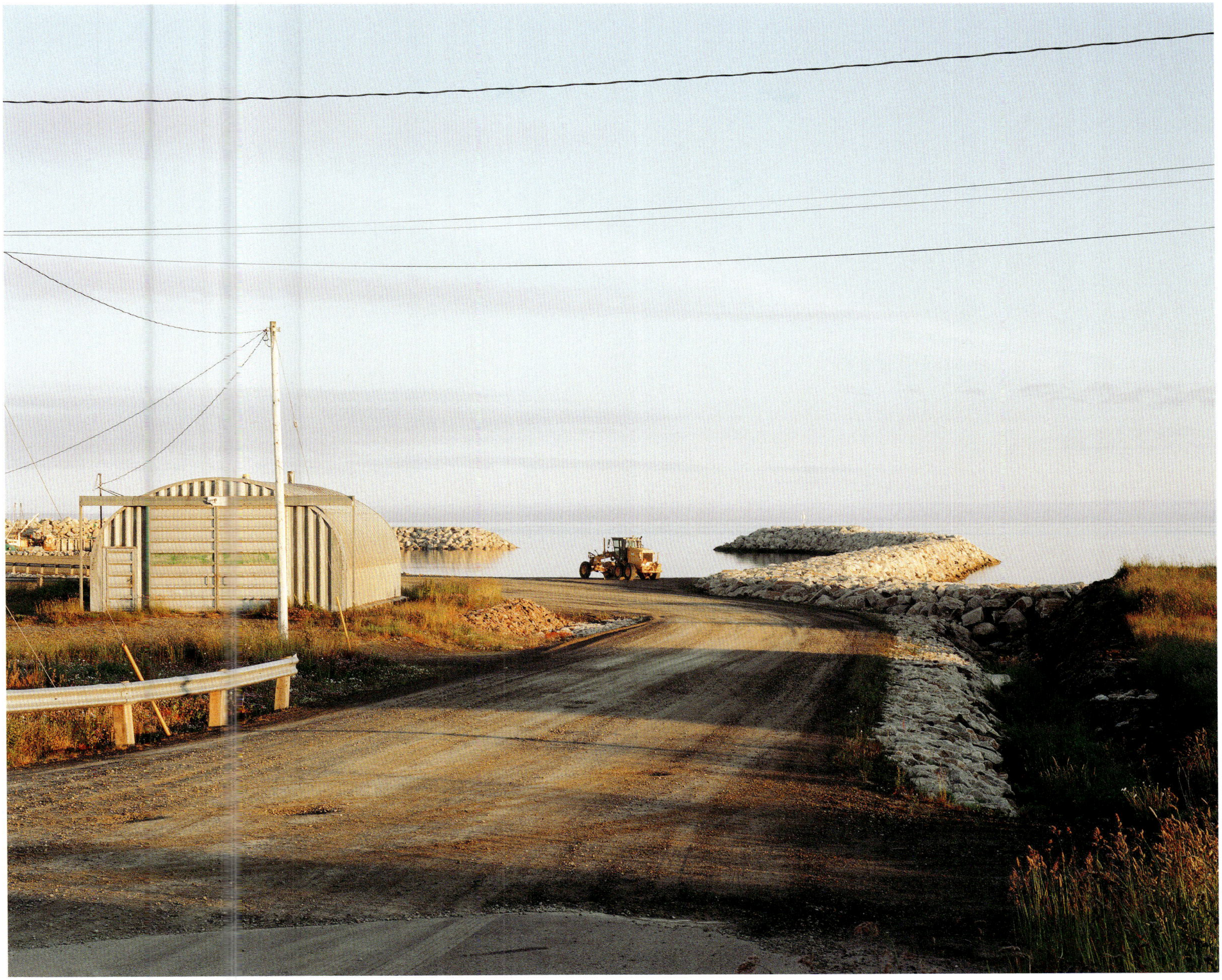

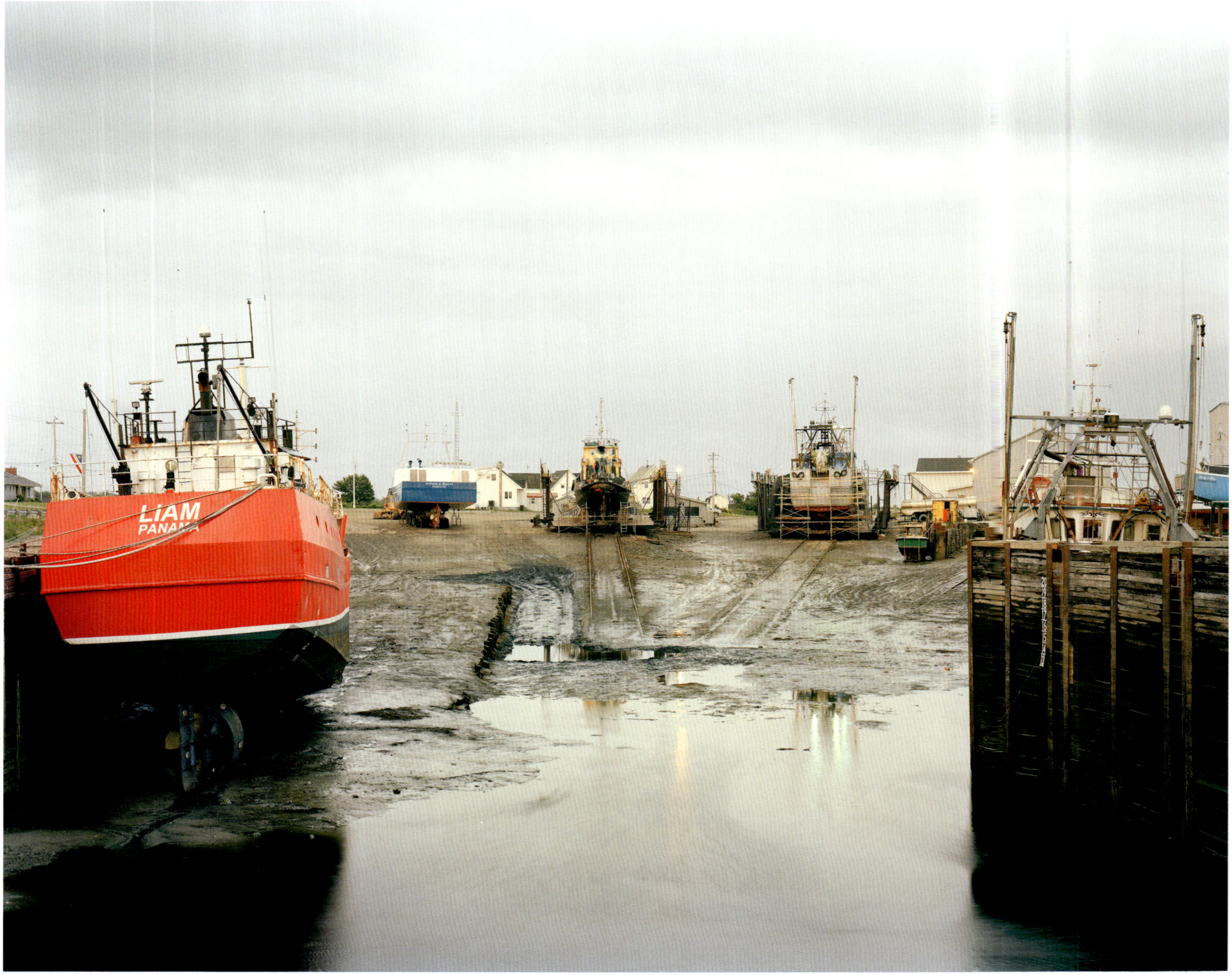
LIAM

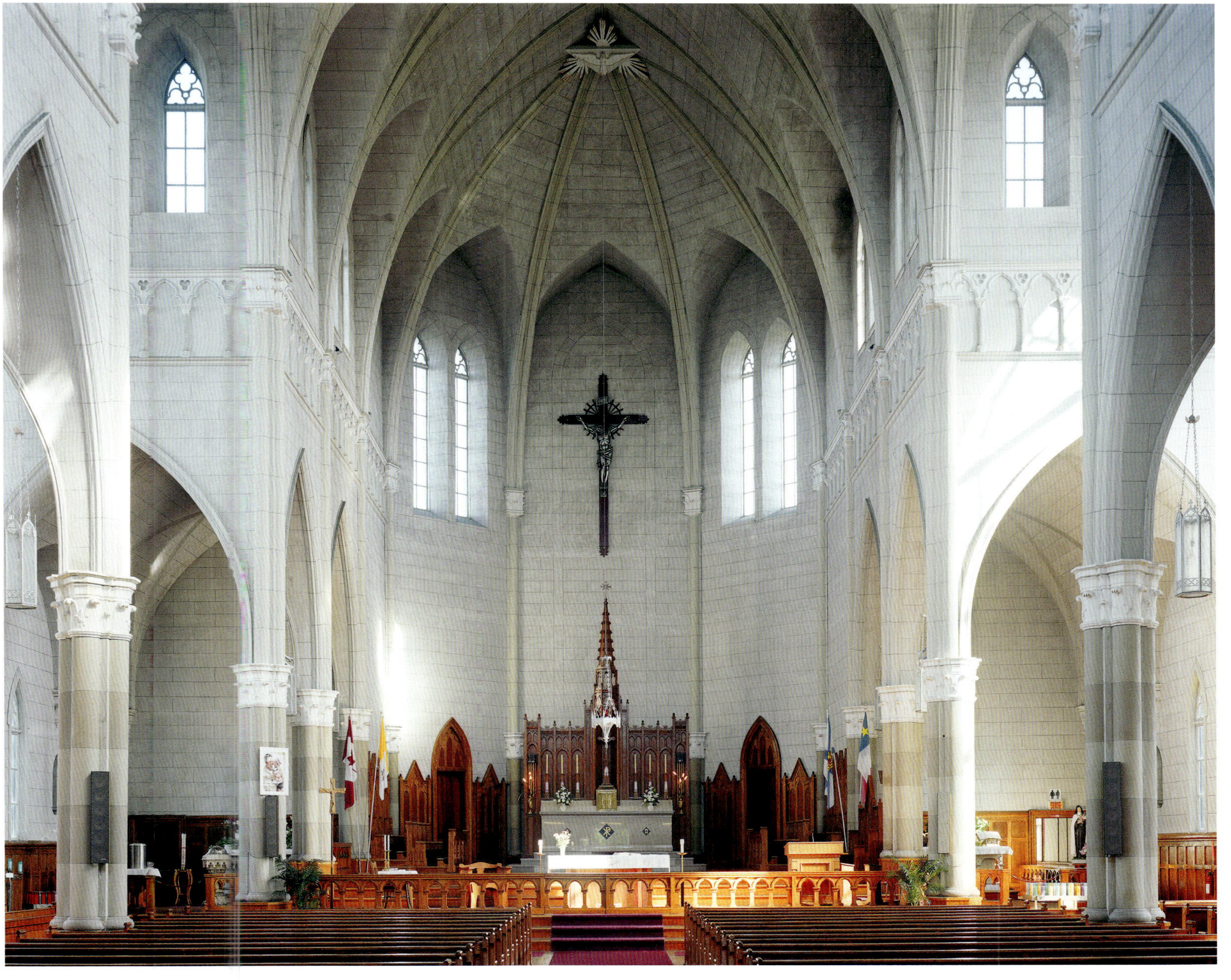

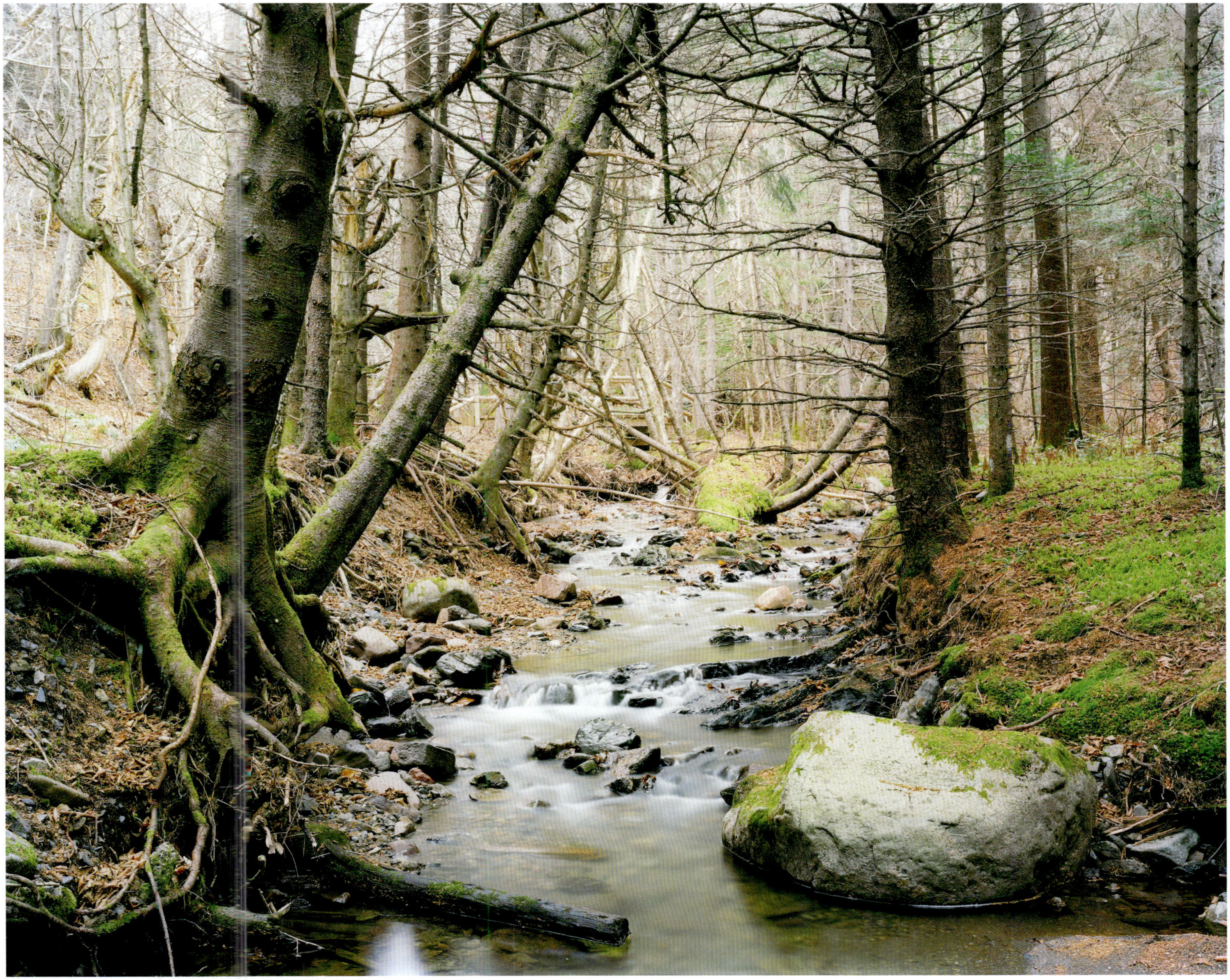

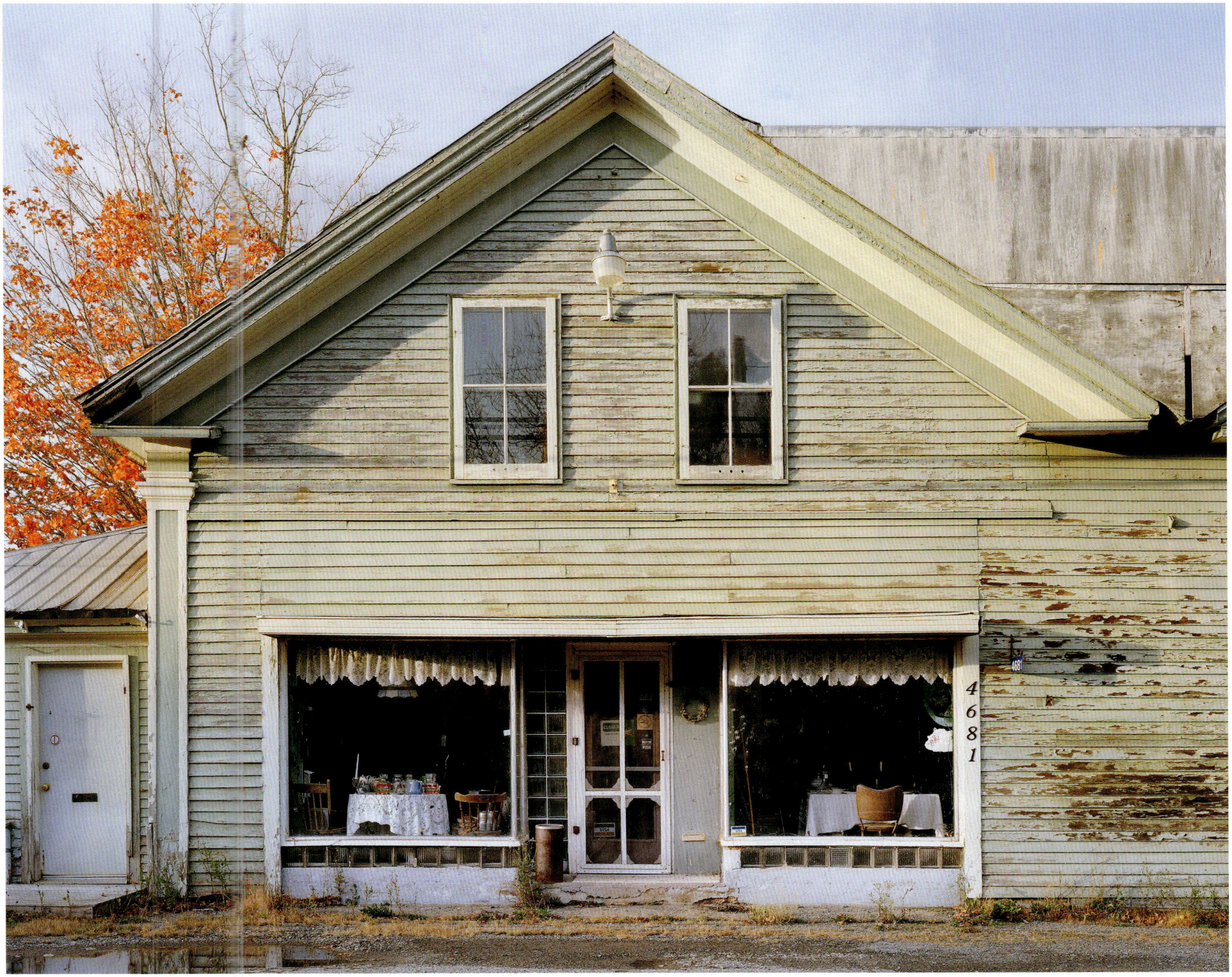
4681

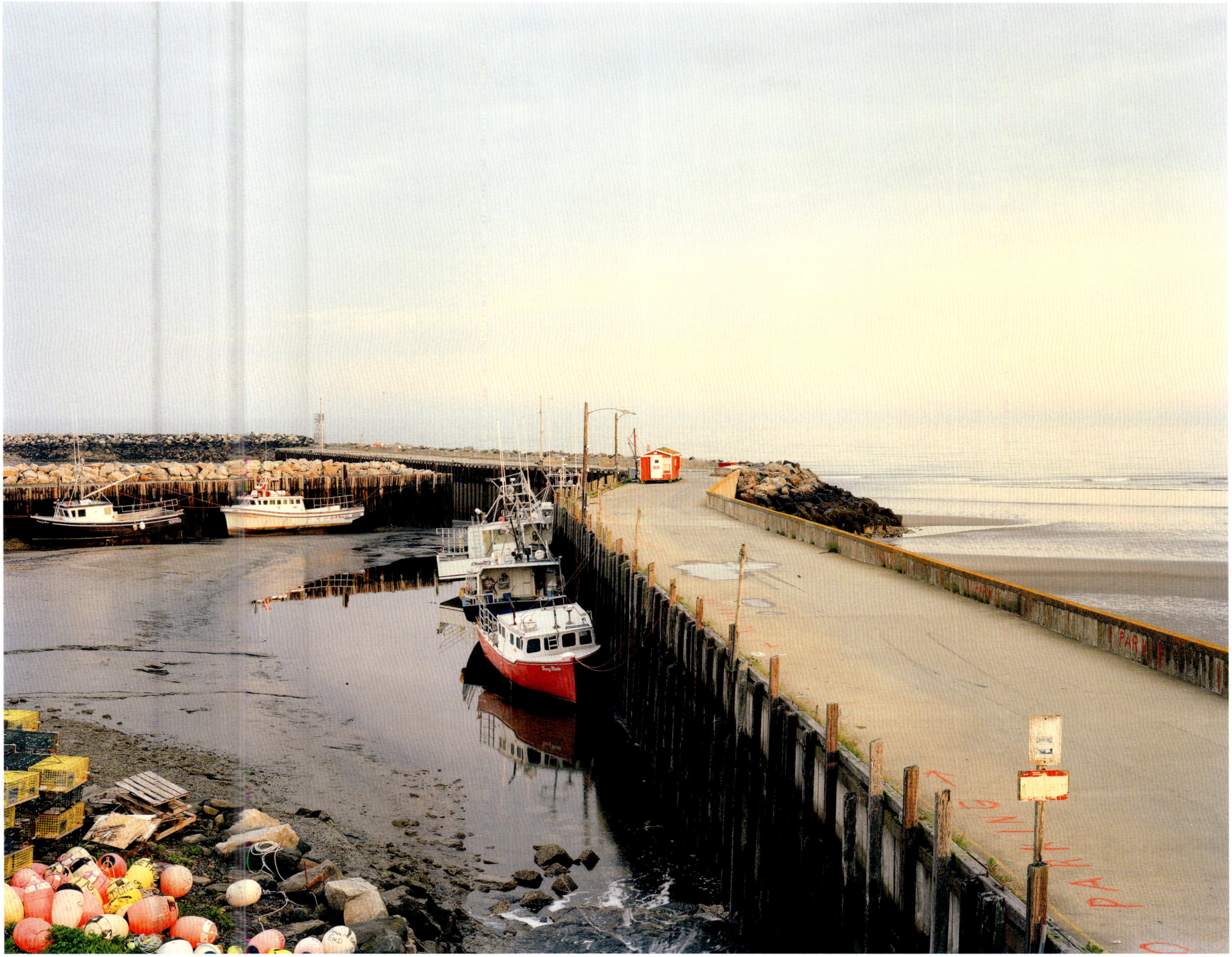

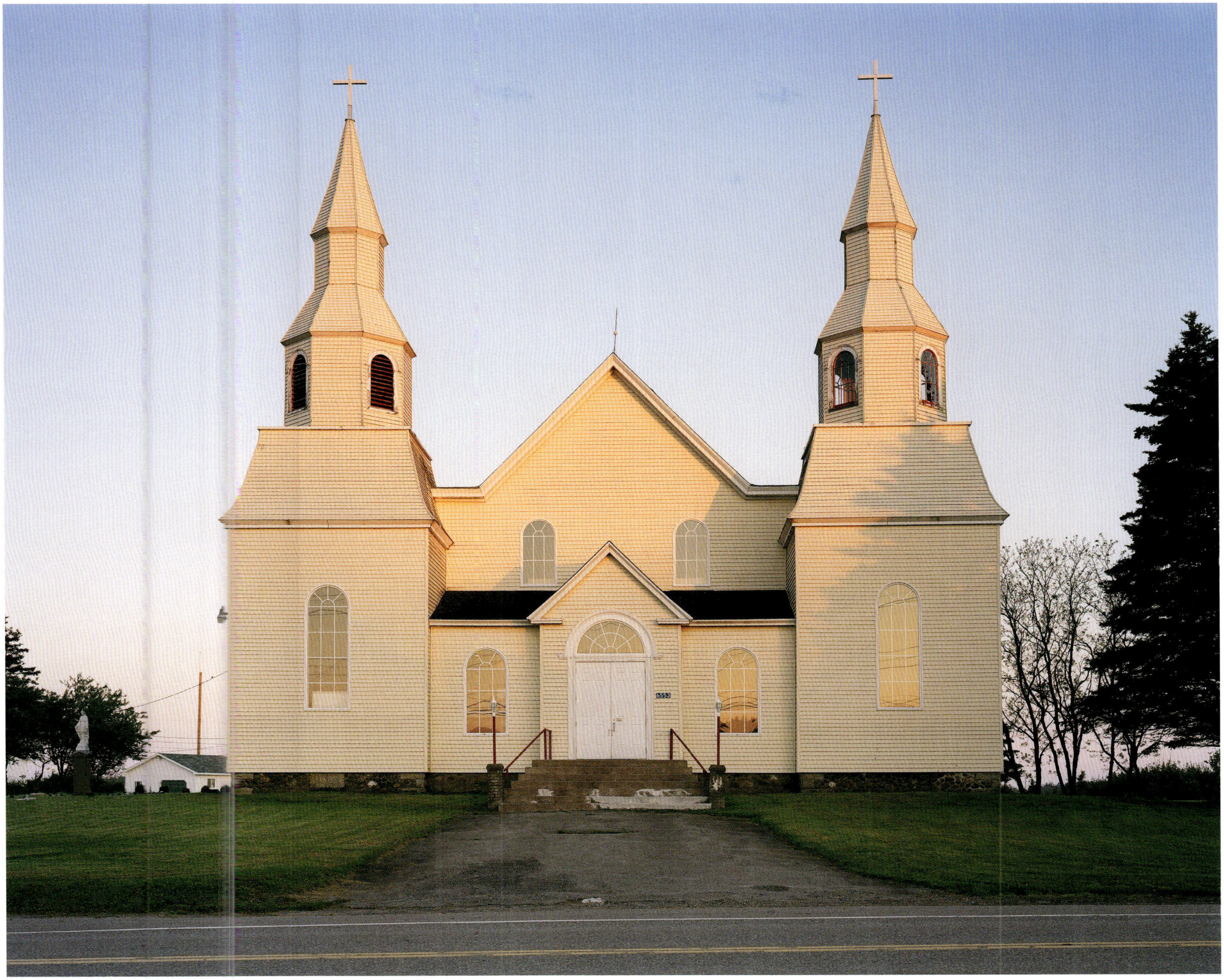

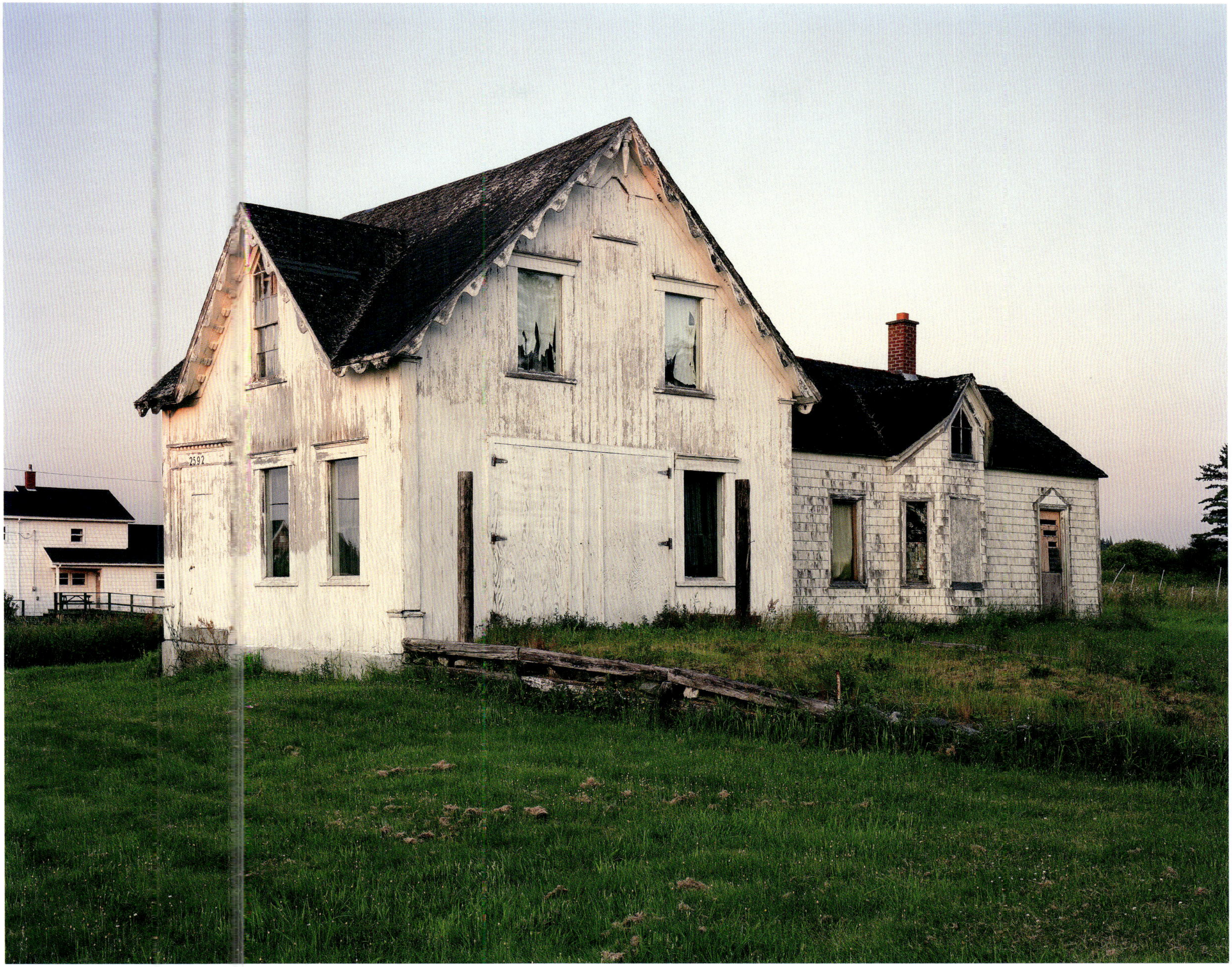

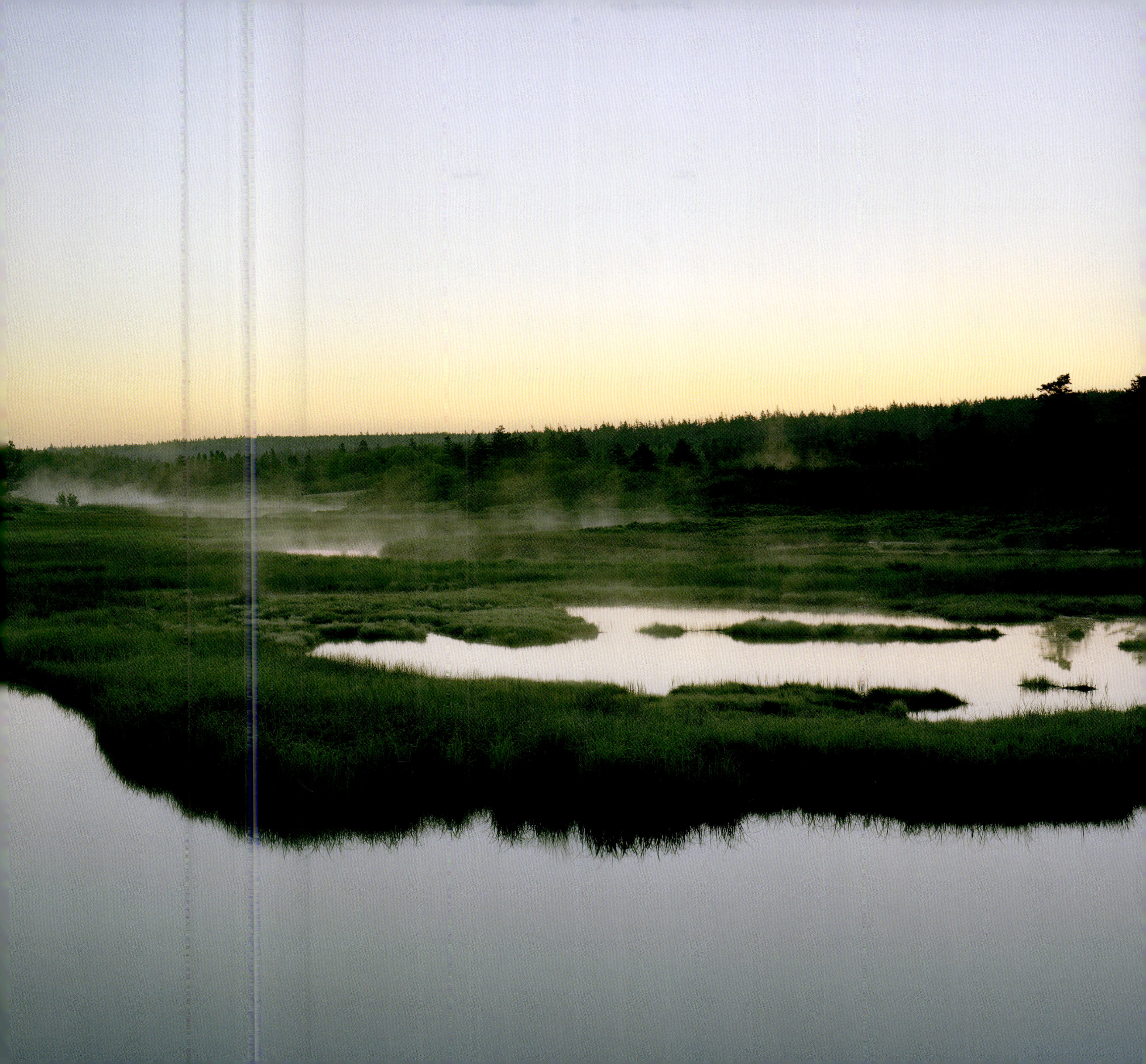

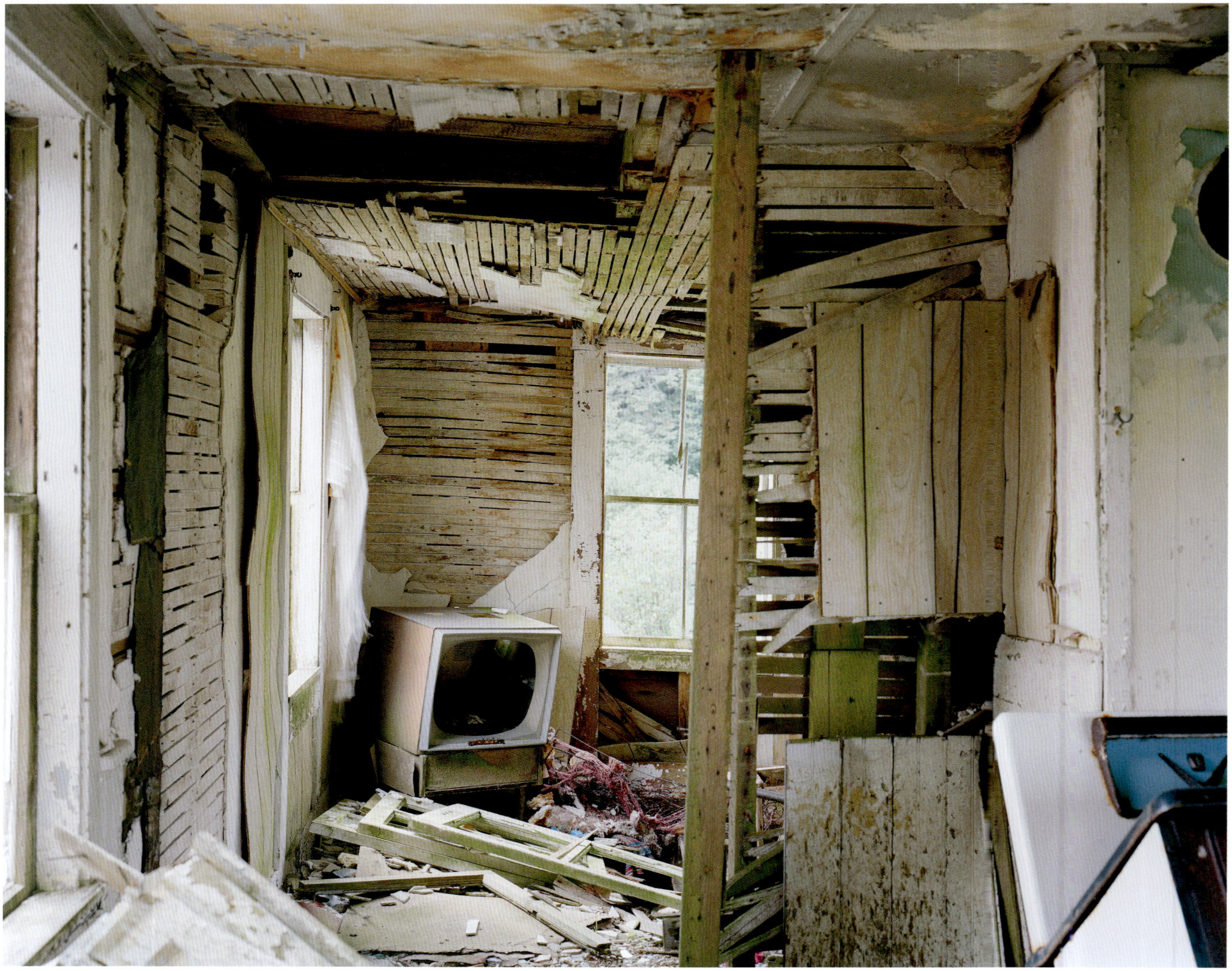

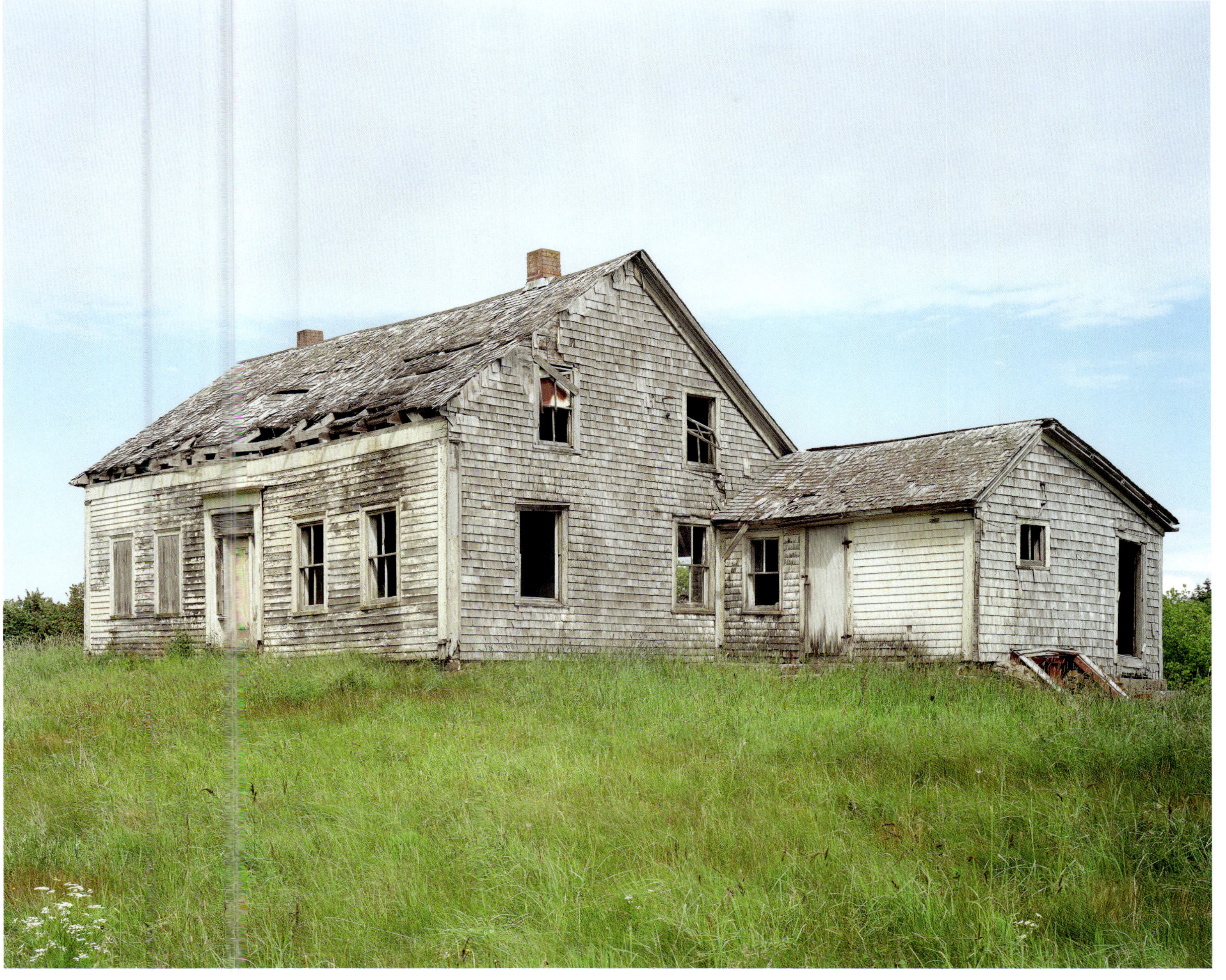

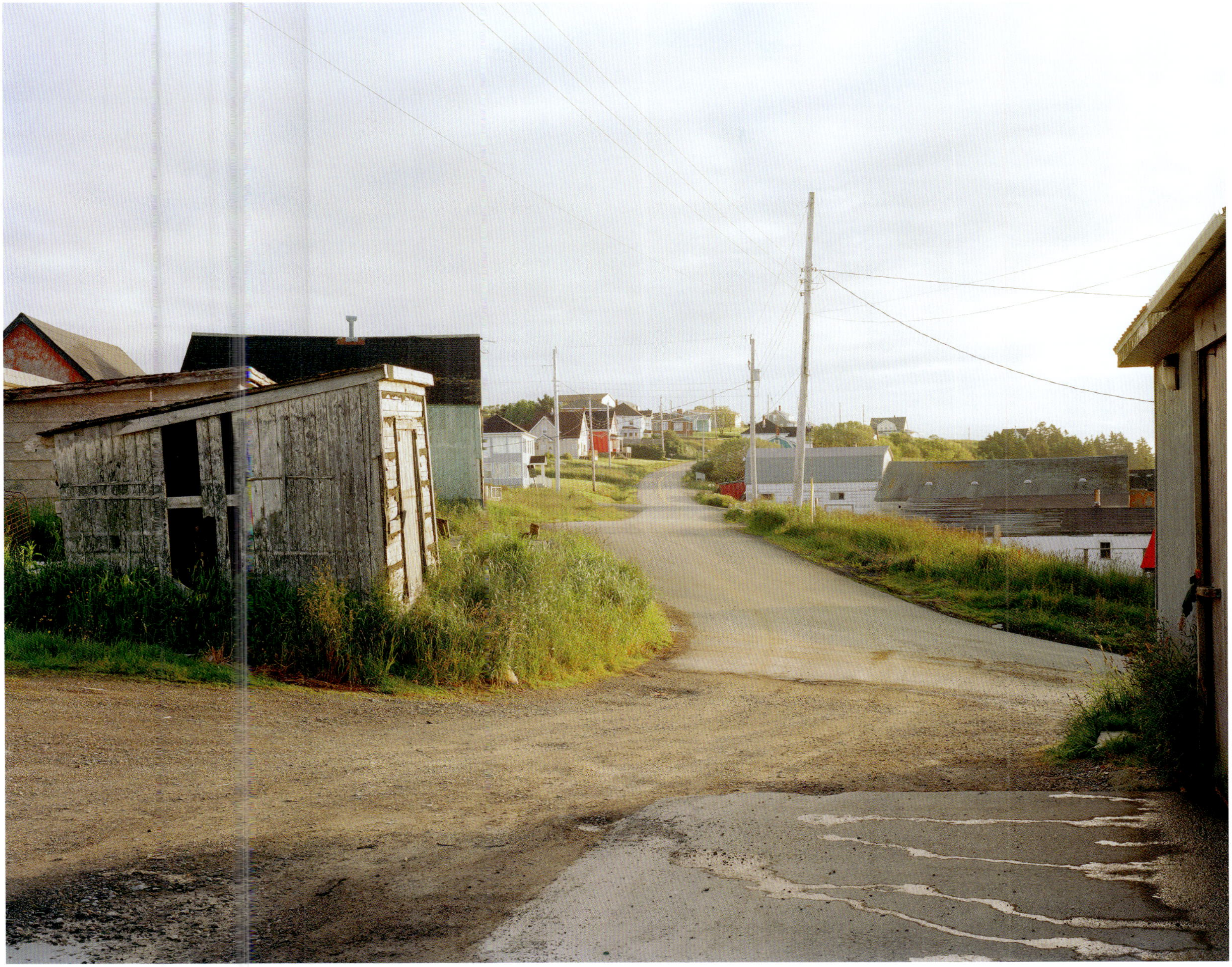

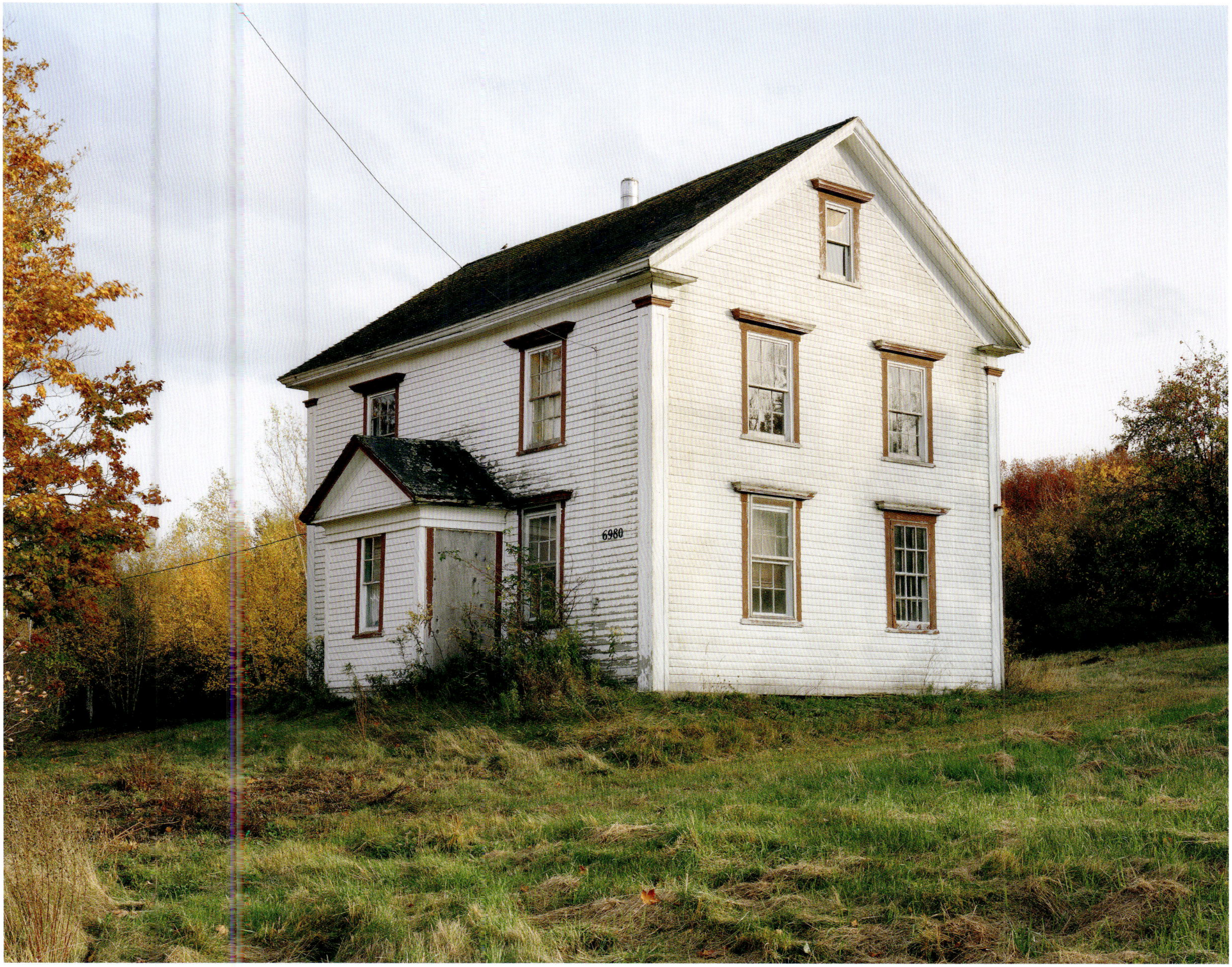
6980

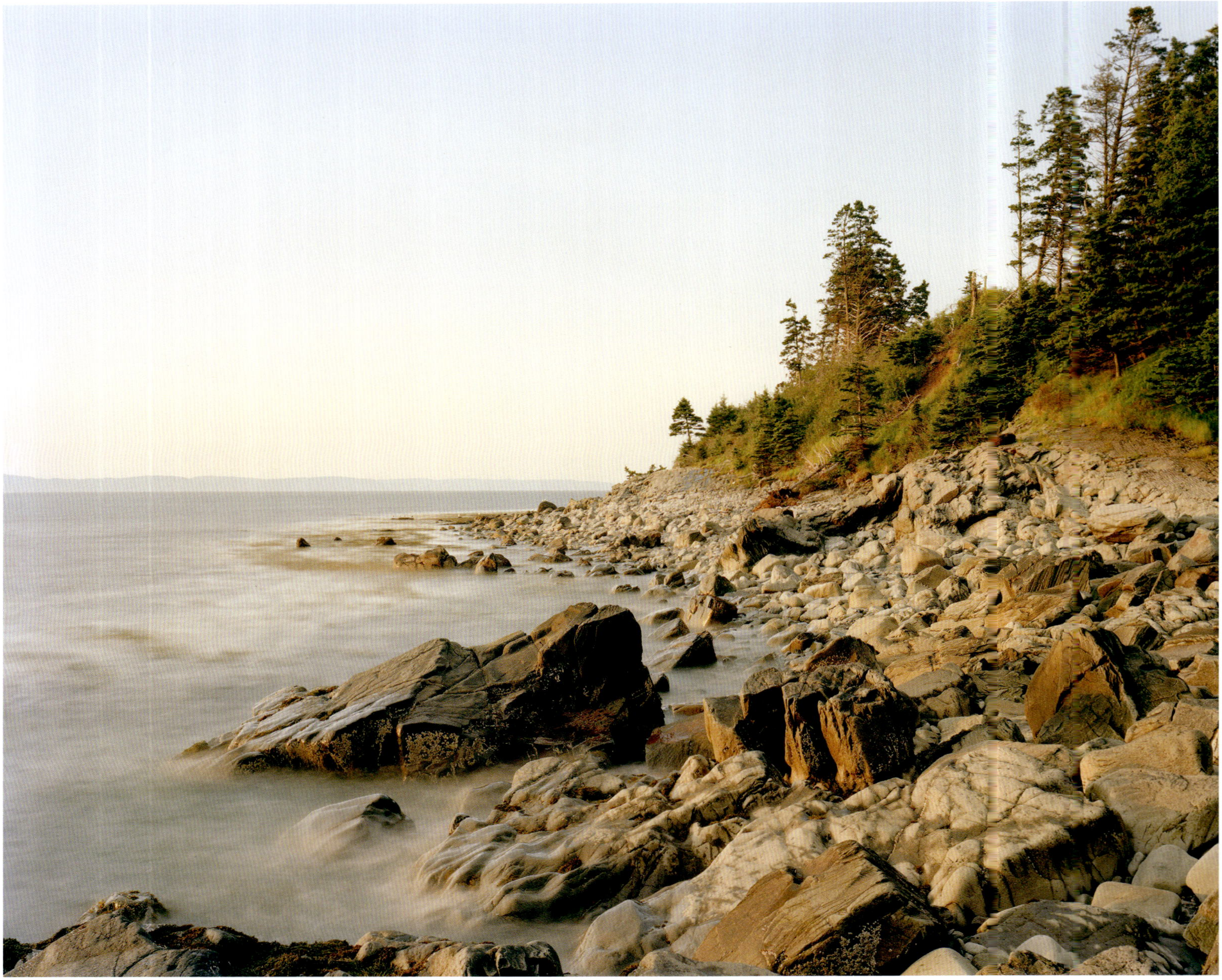

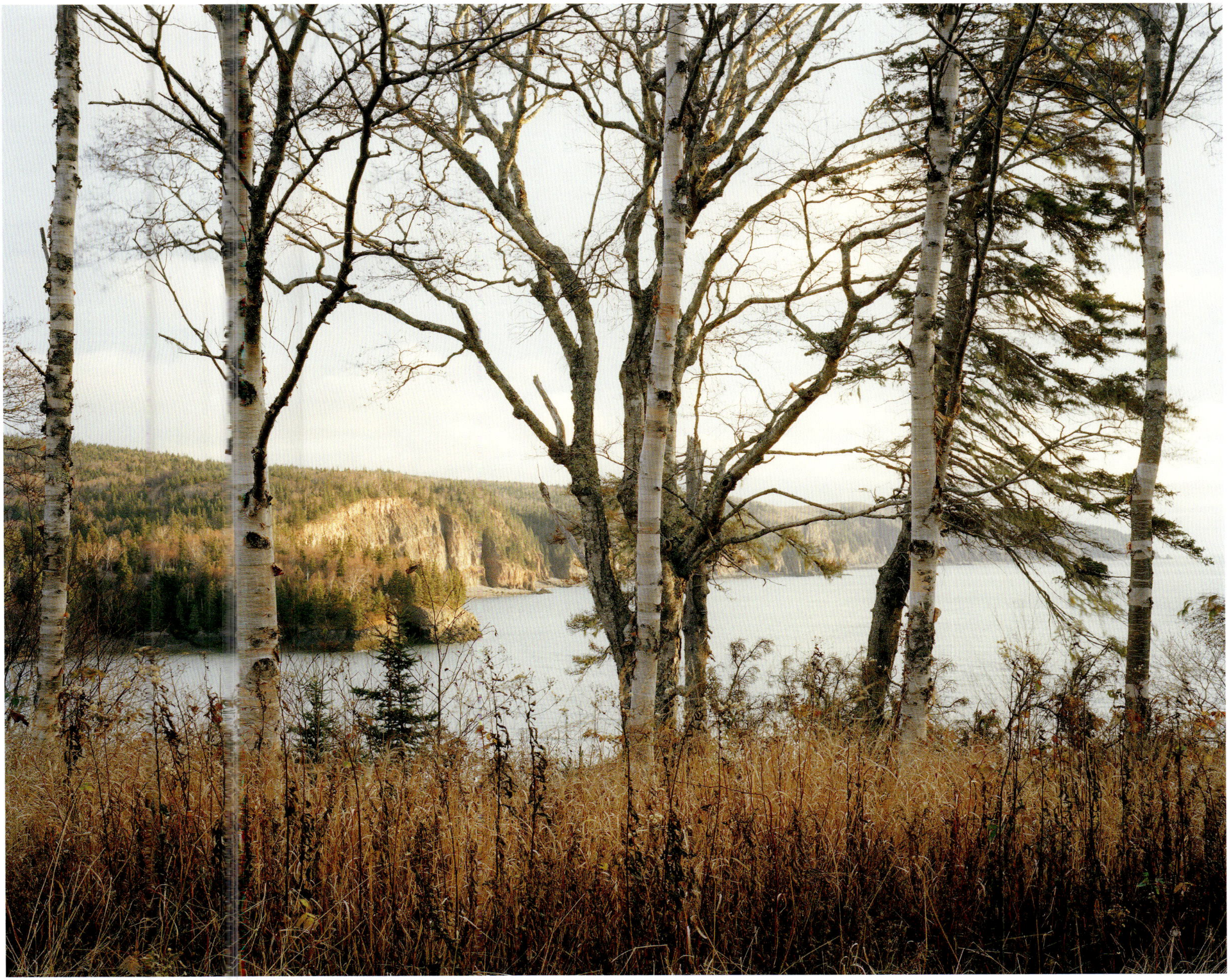

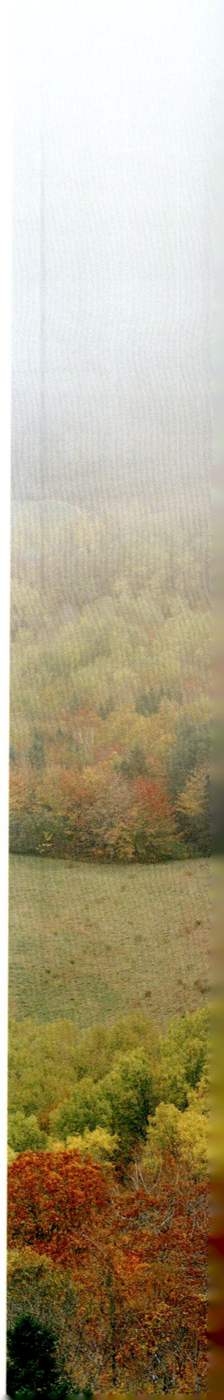

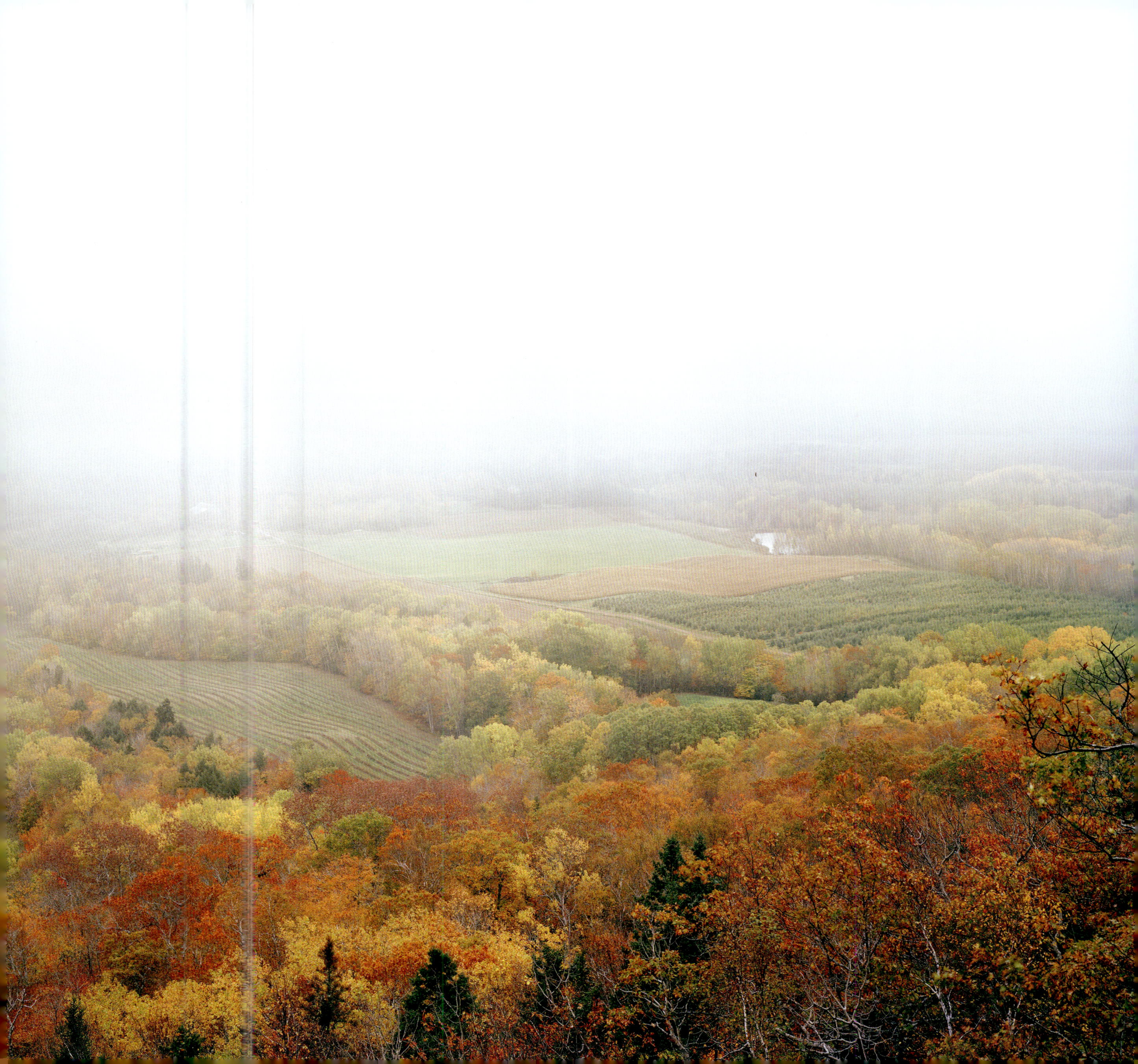

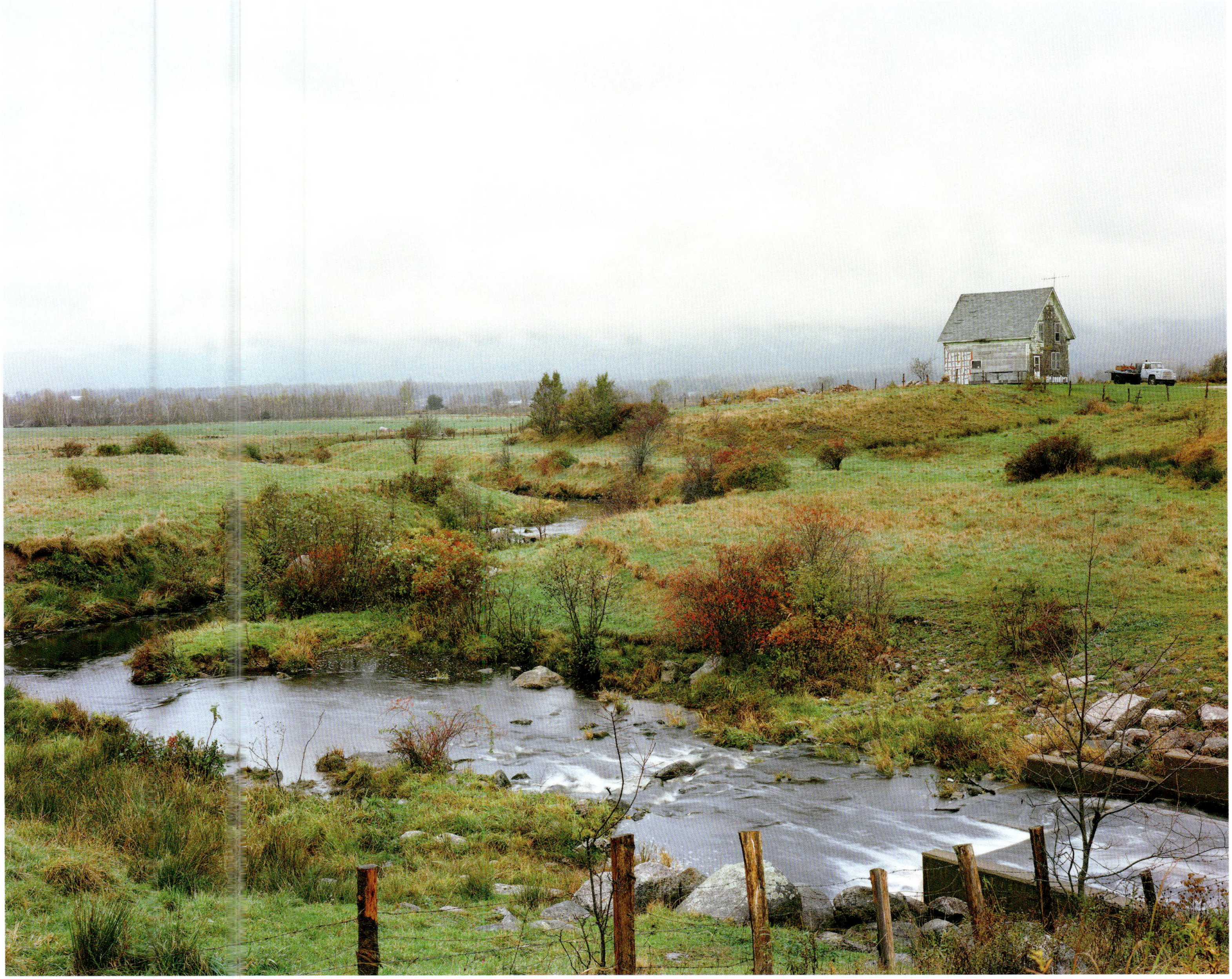

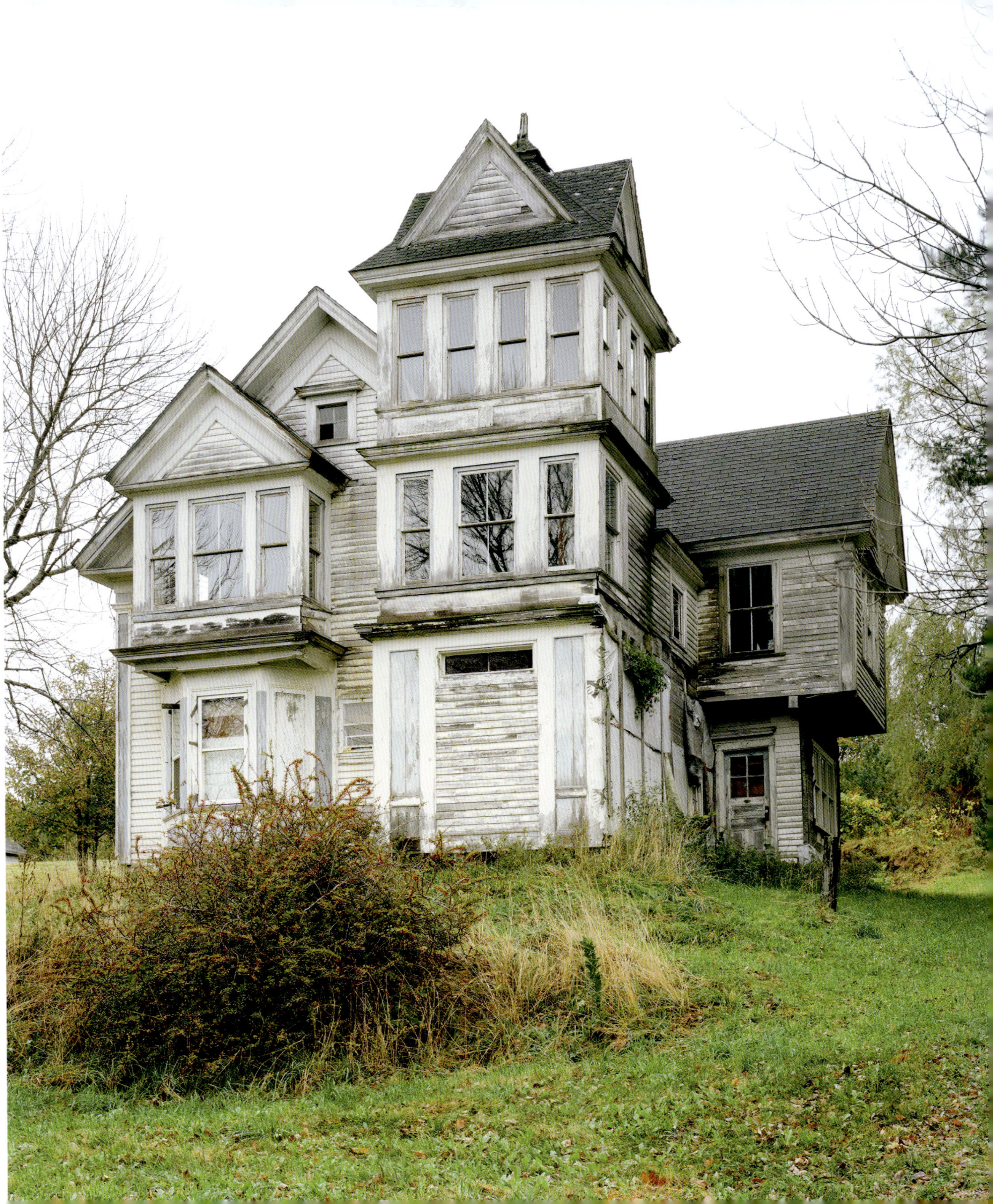

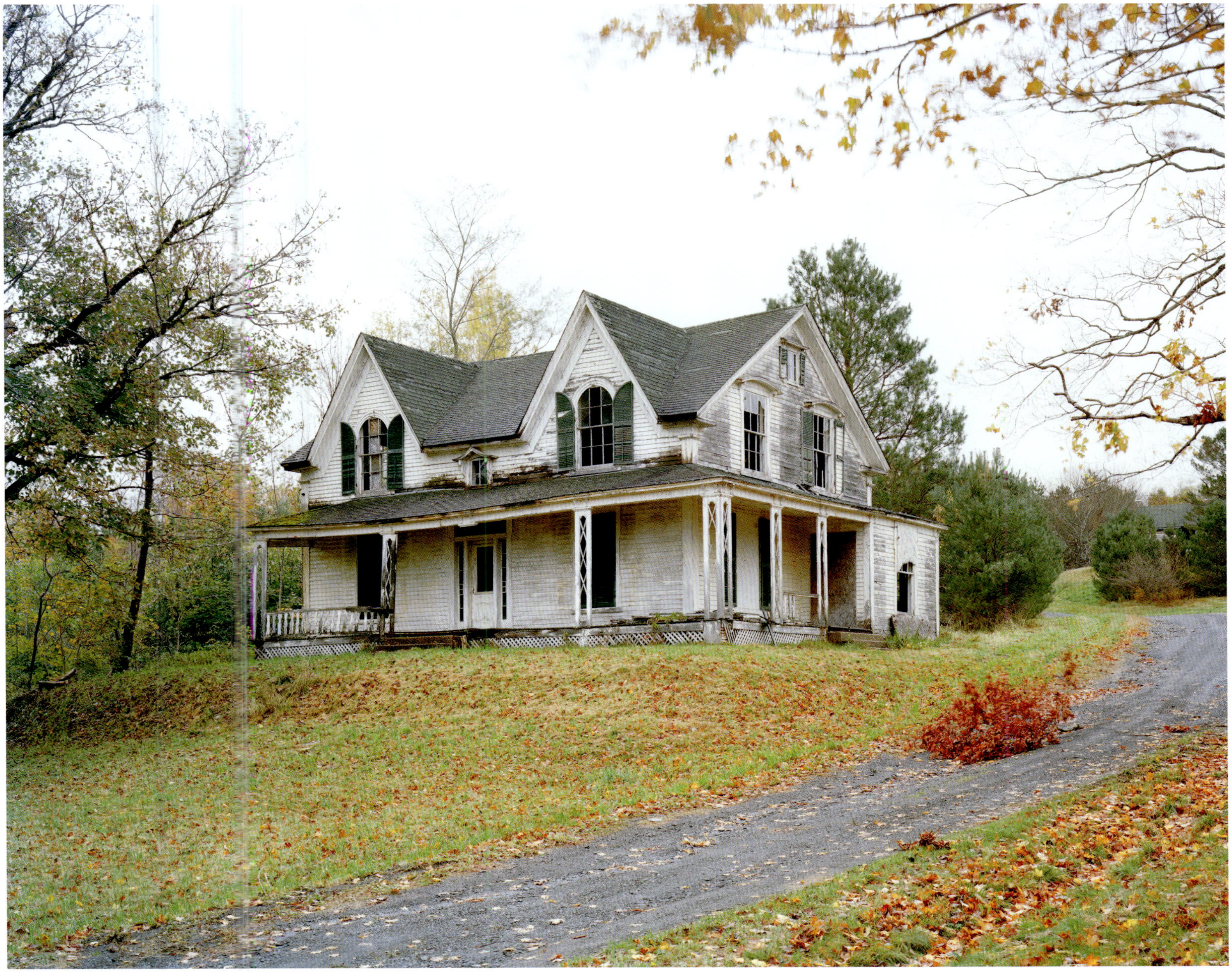

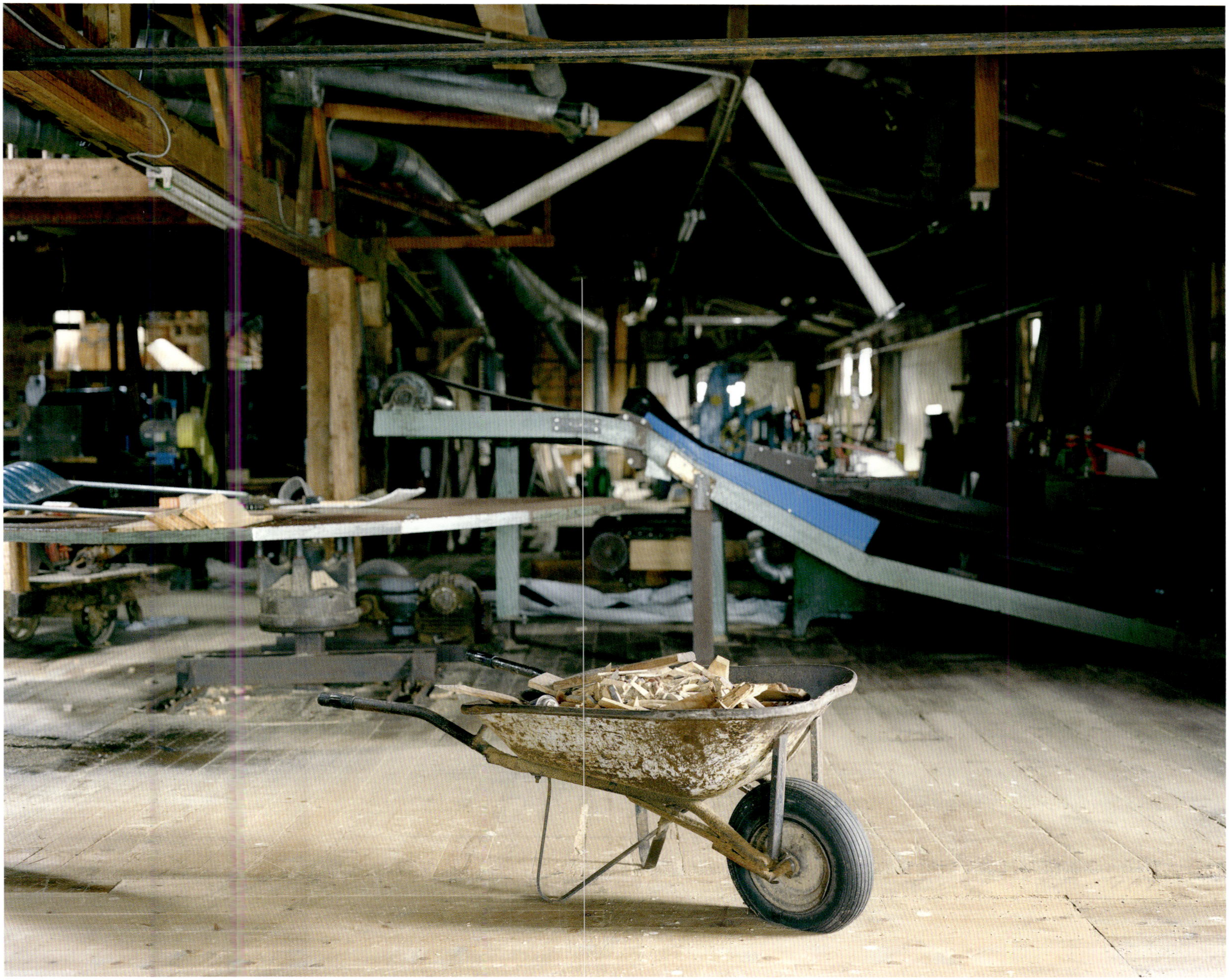

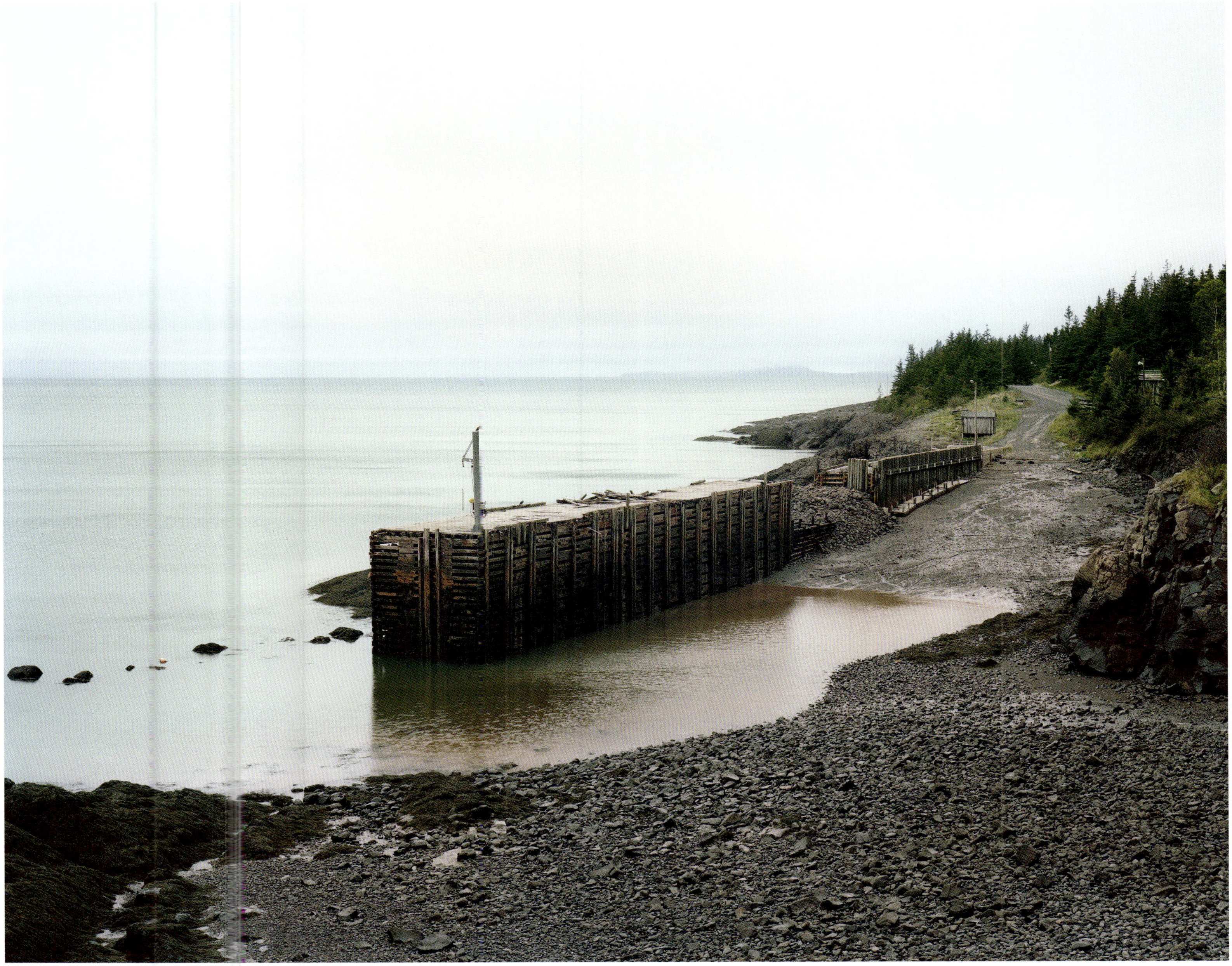

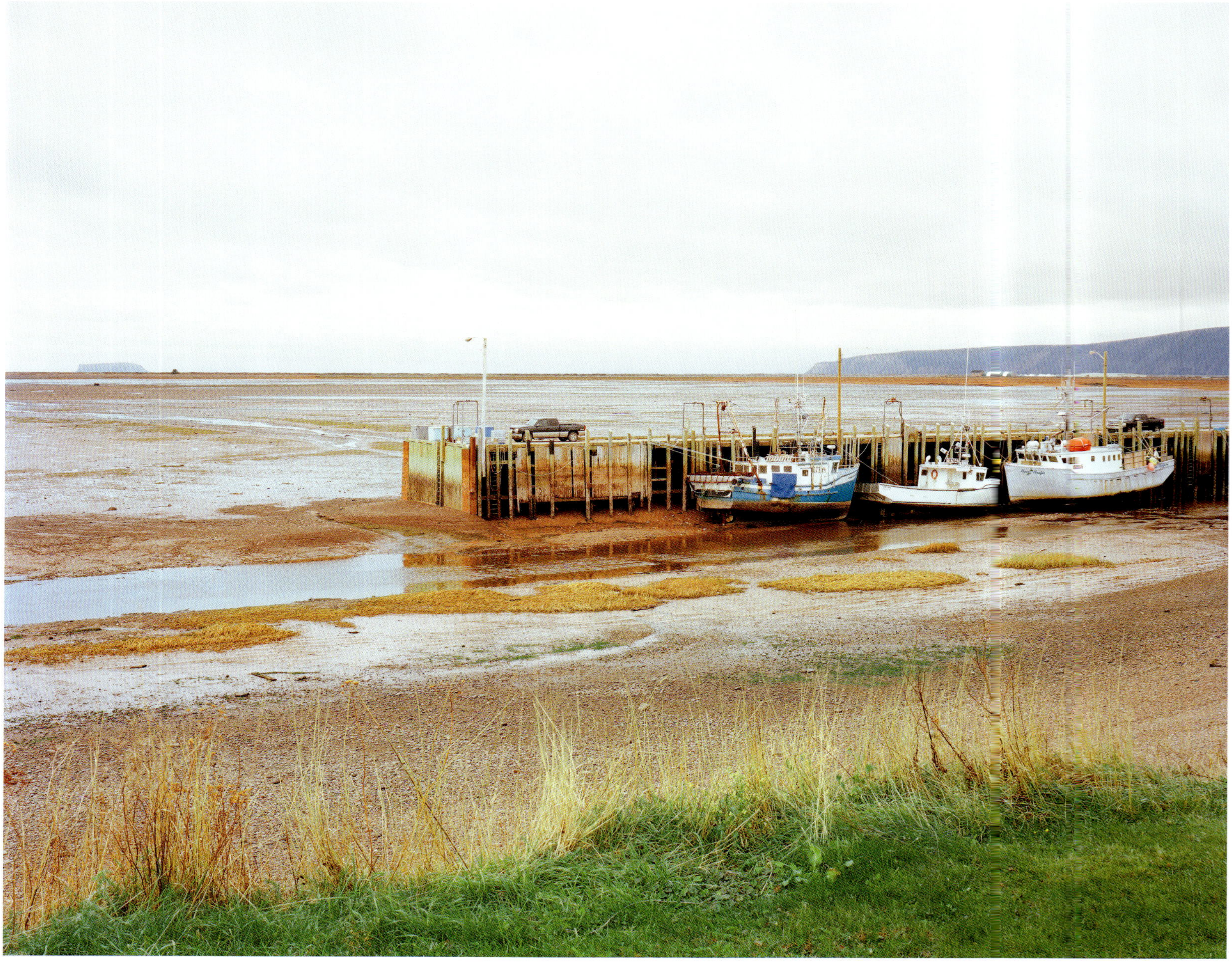

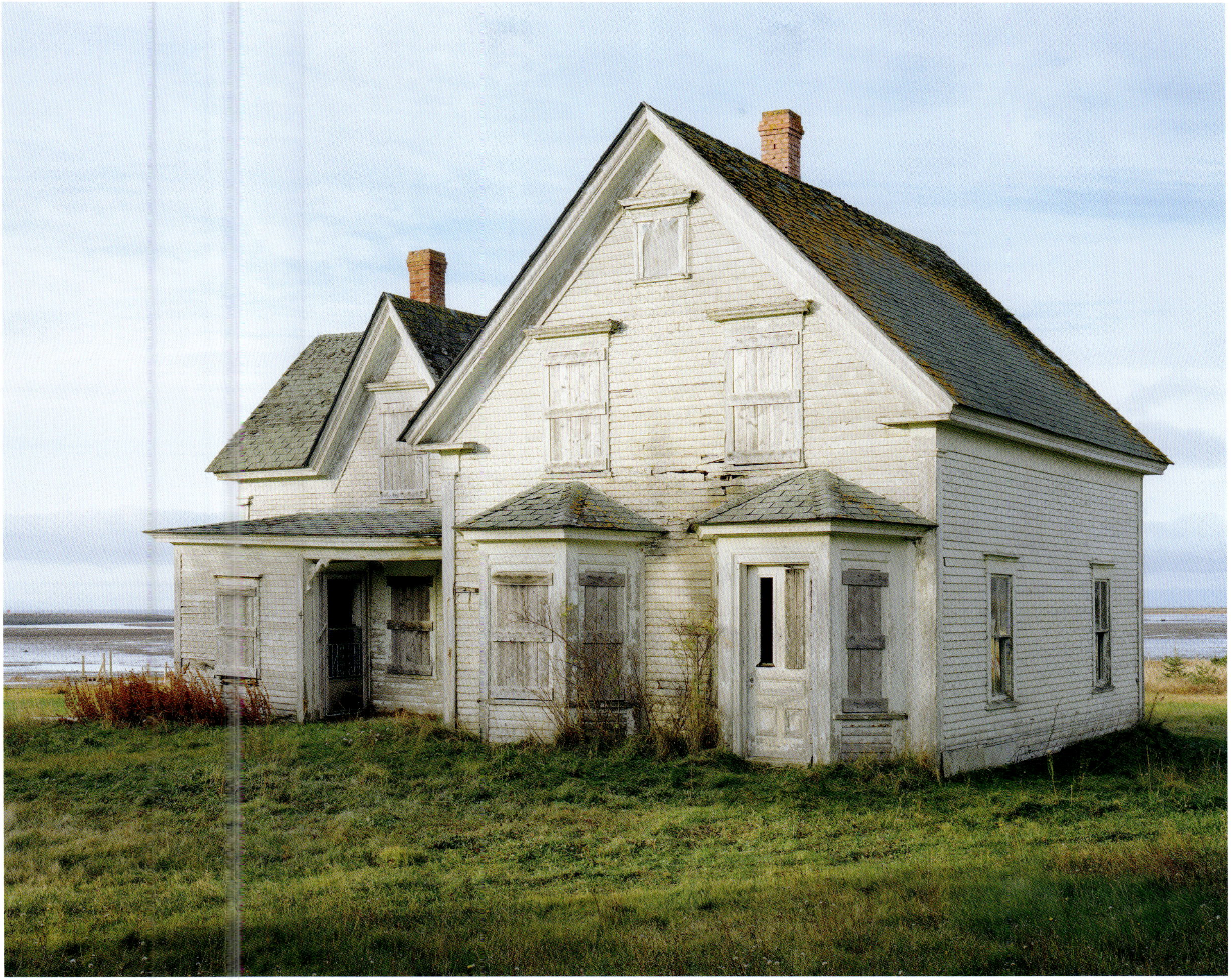

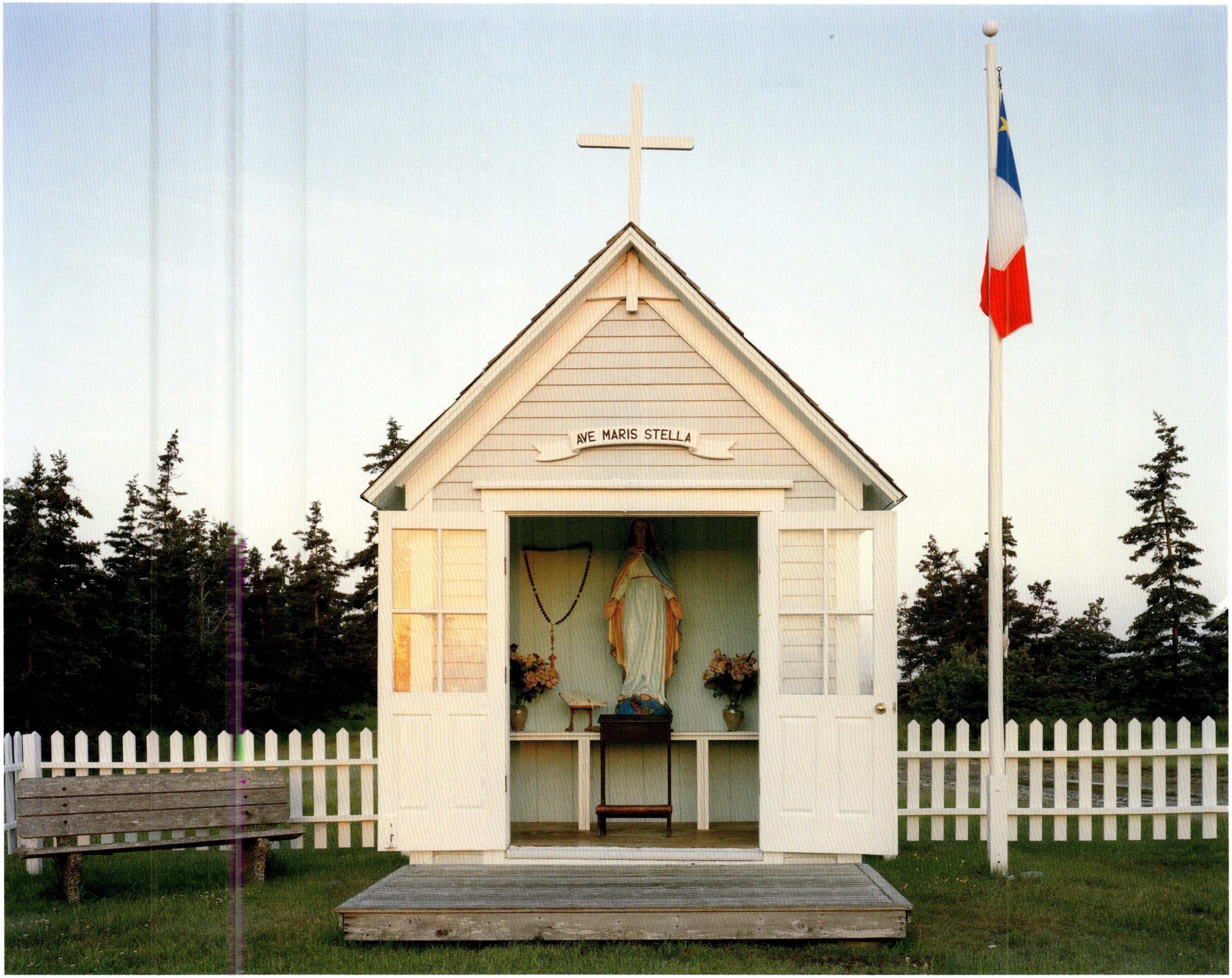
AVE MARIS STELLA

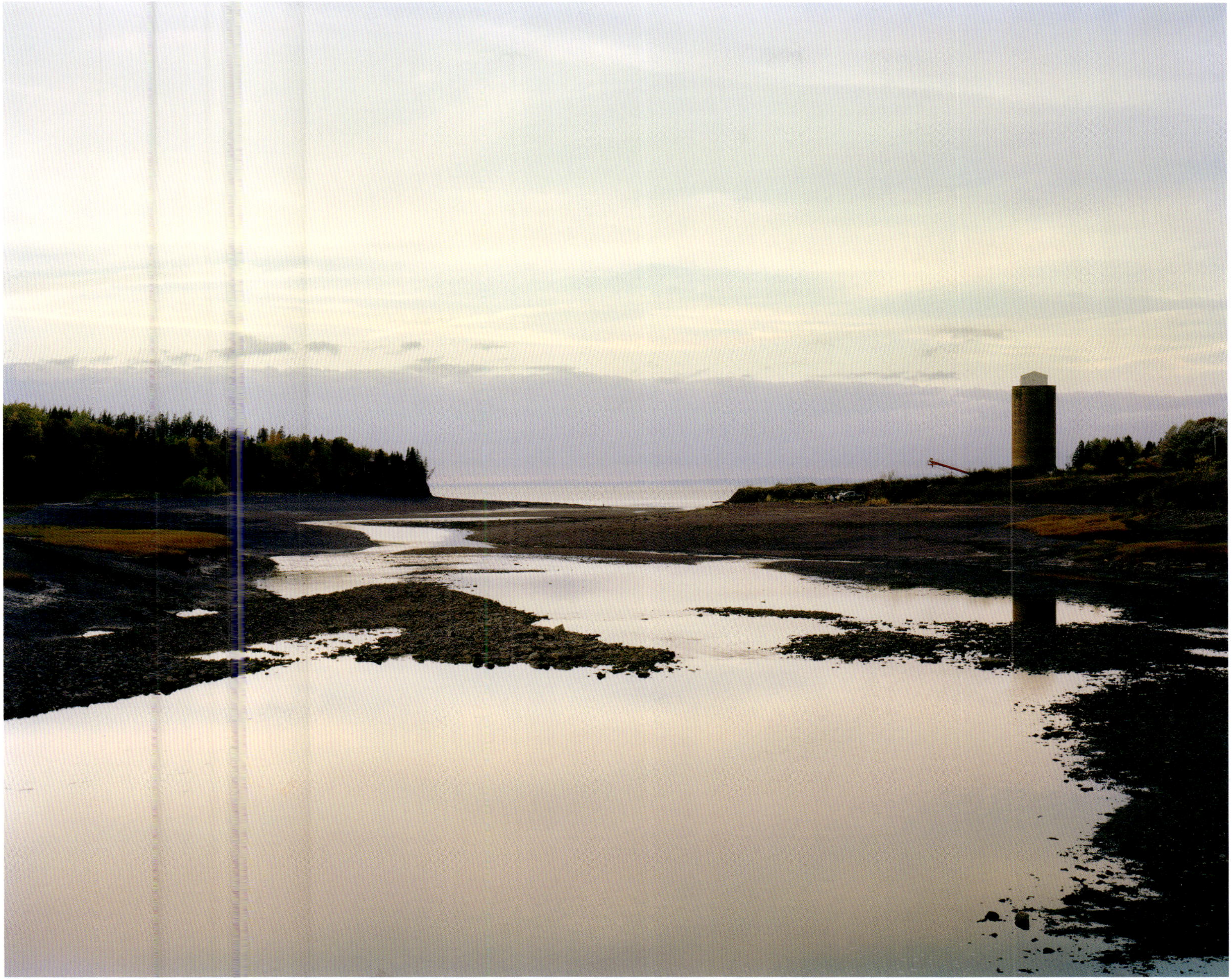

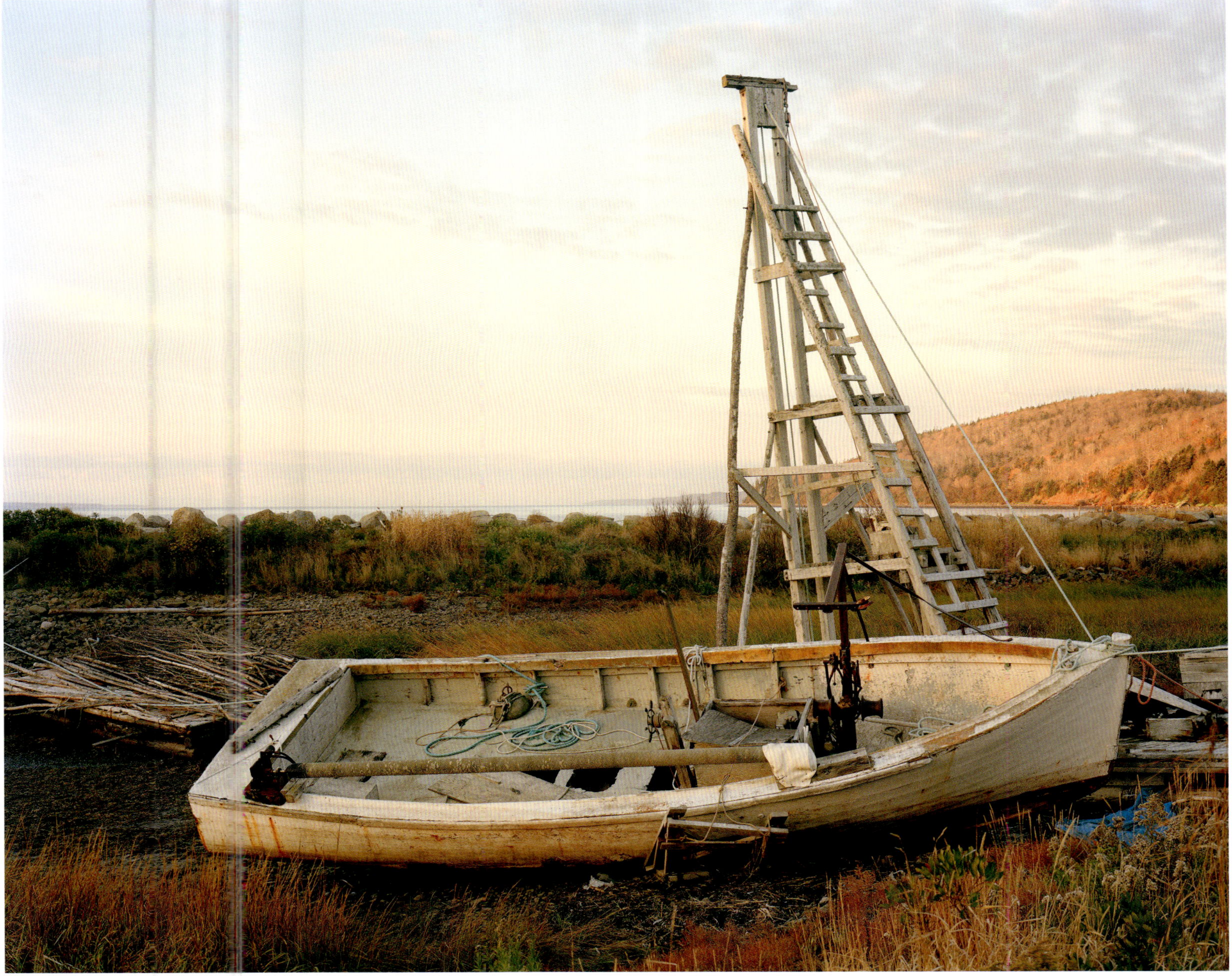

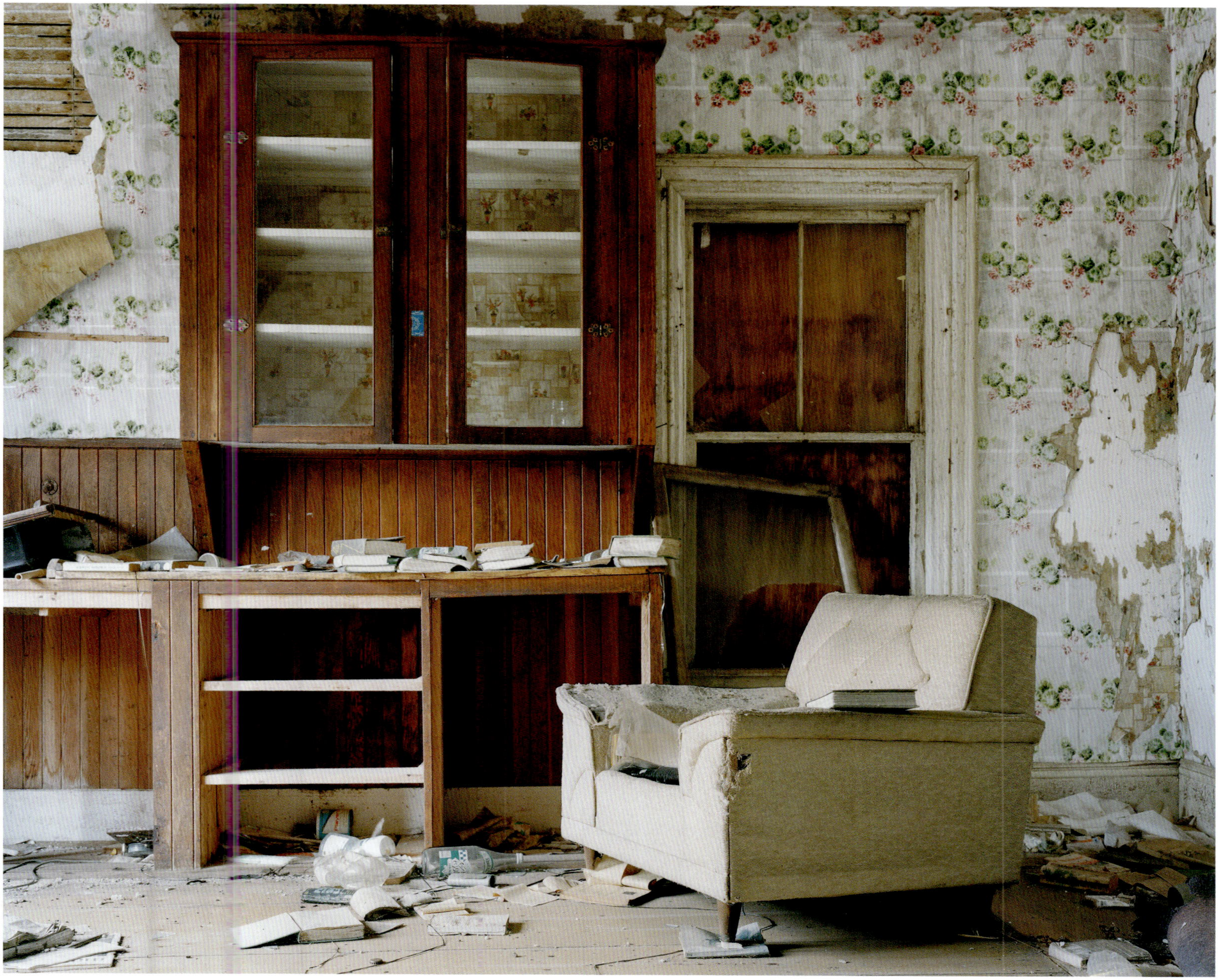

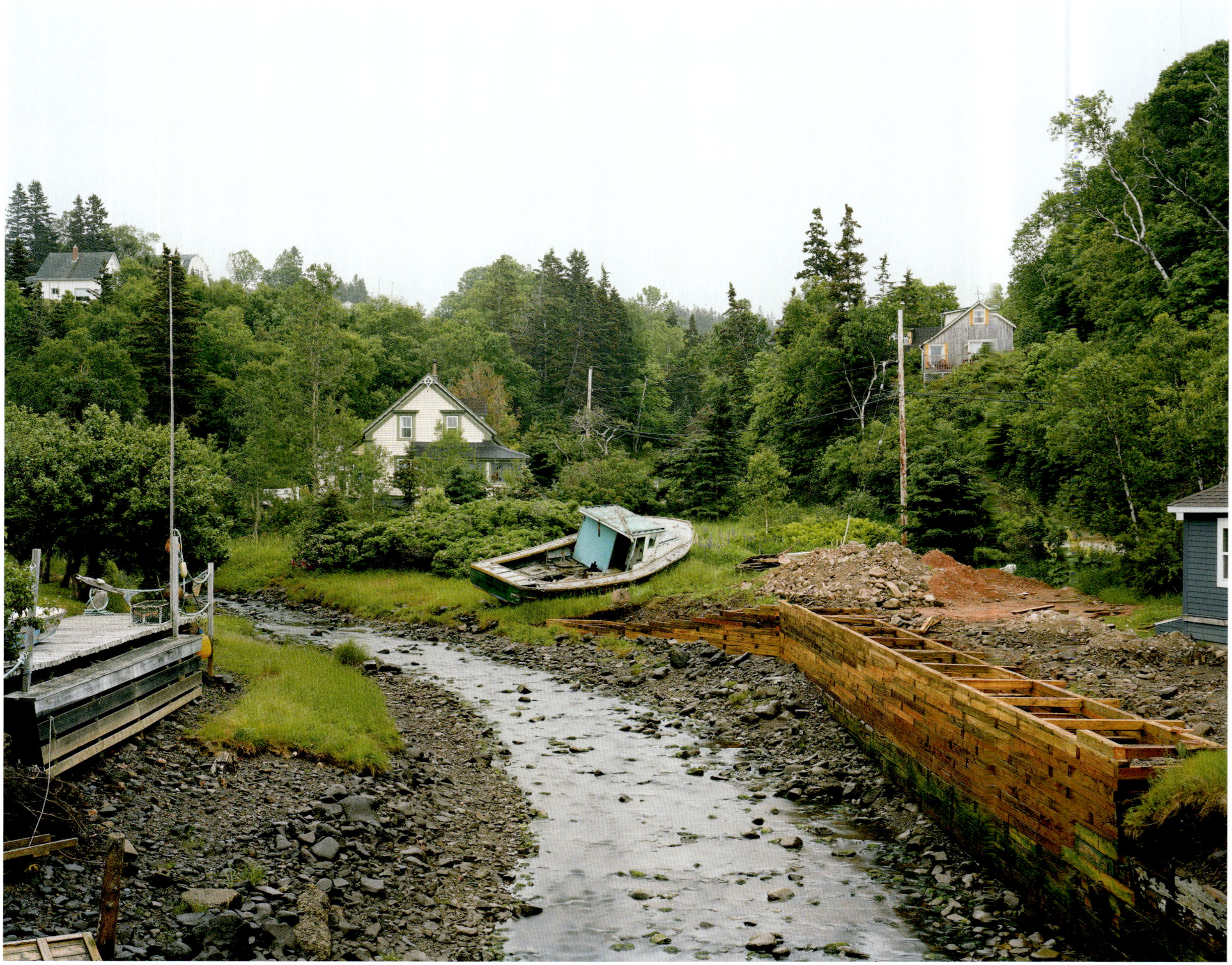

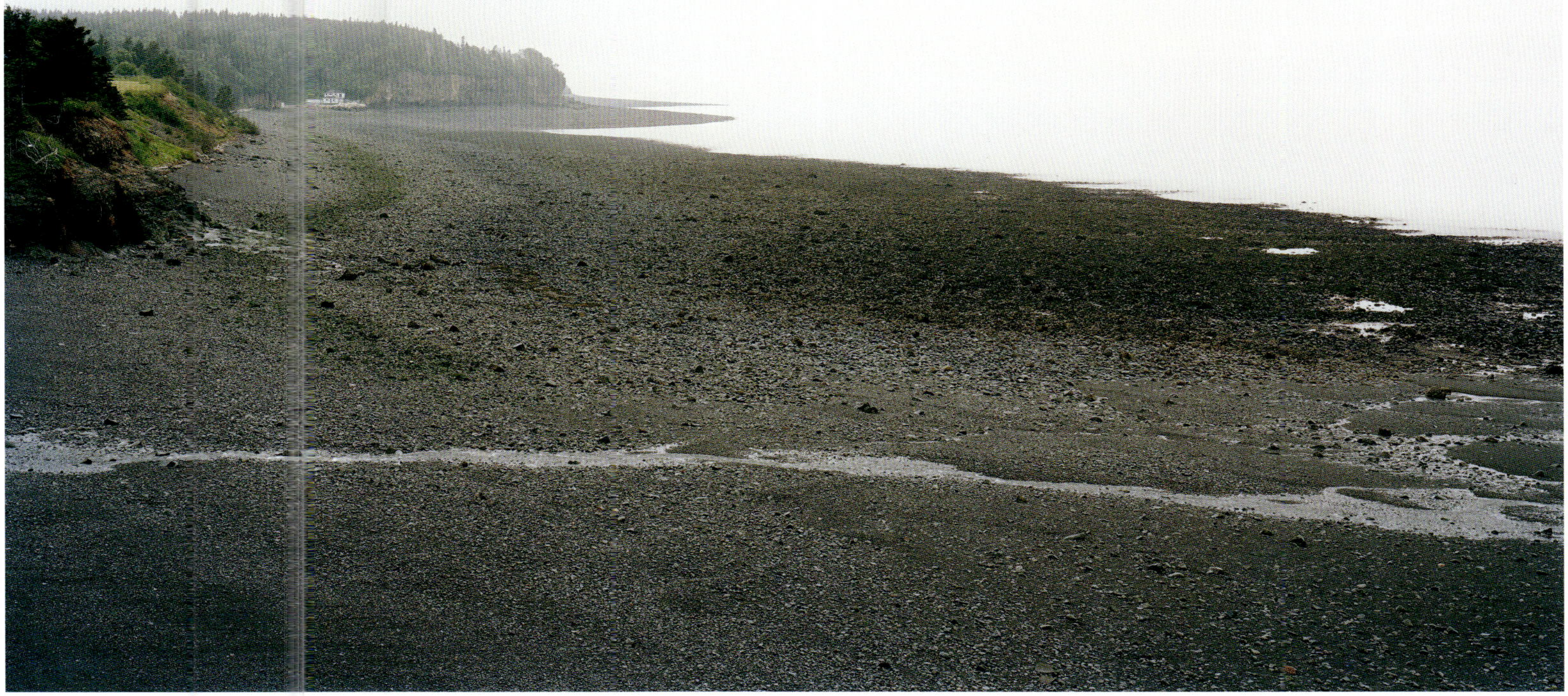

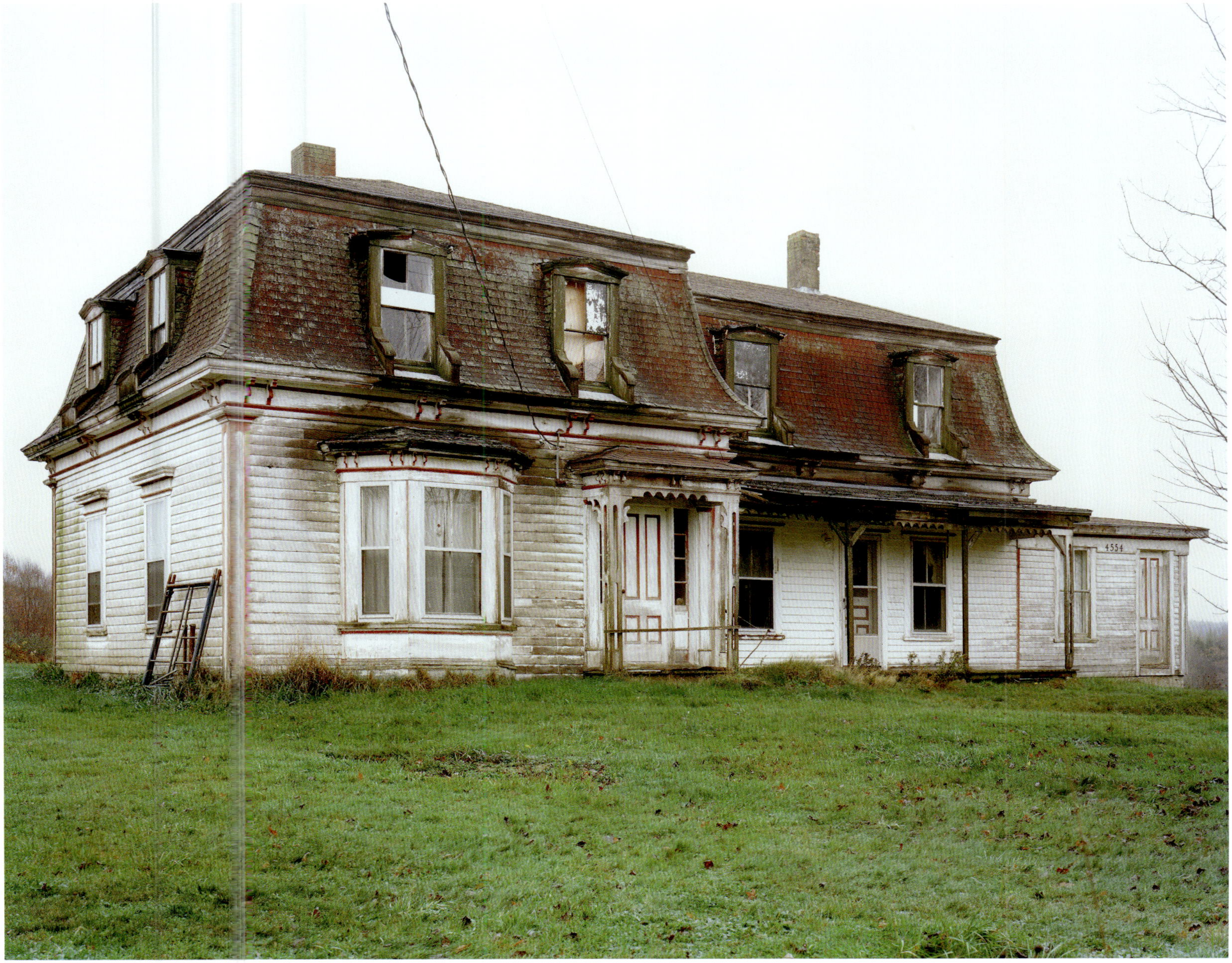
4554

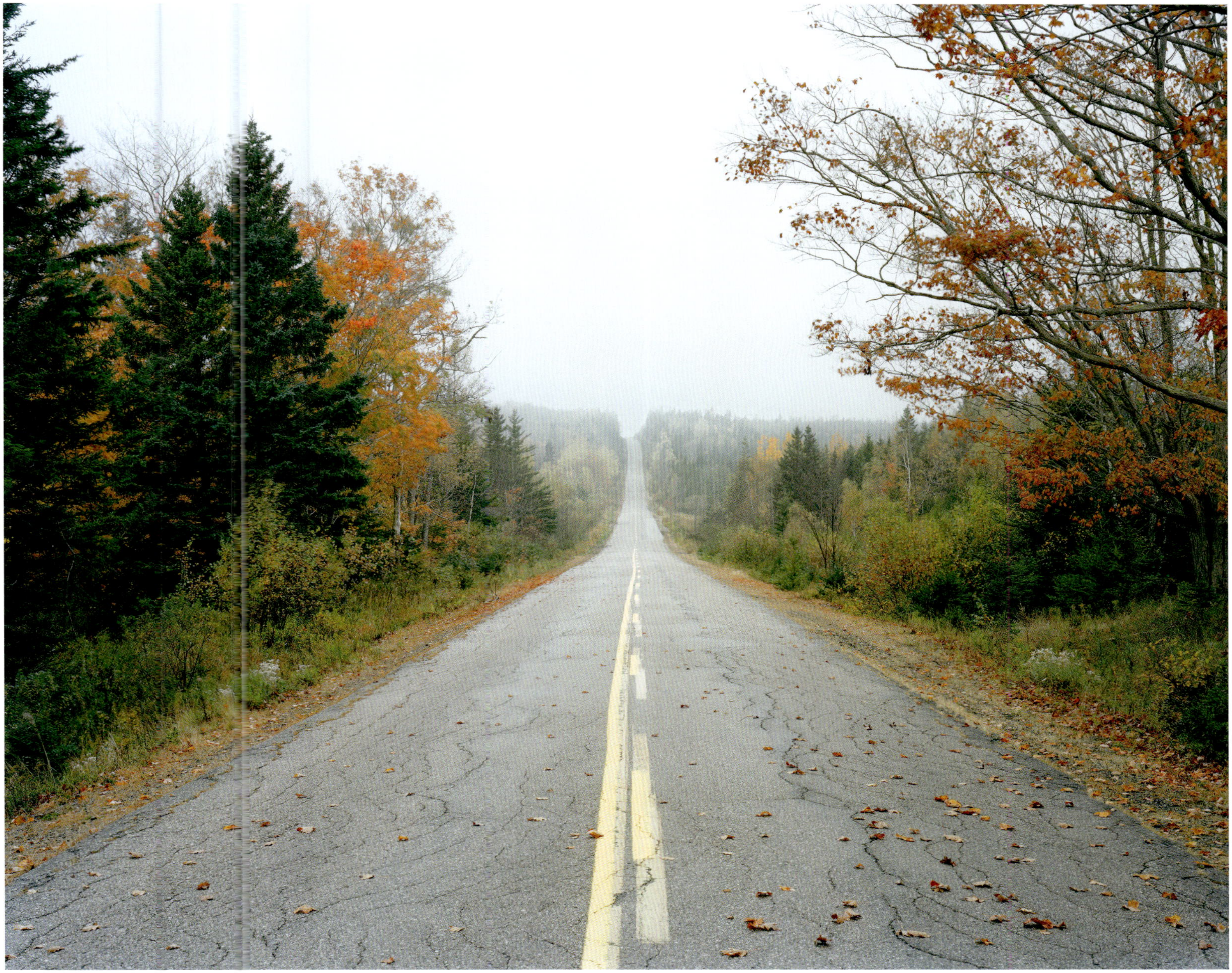

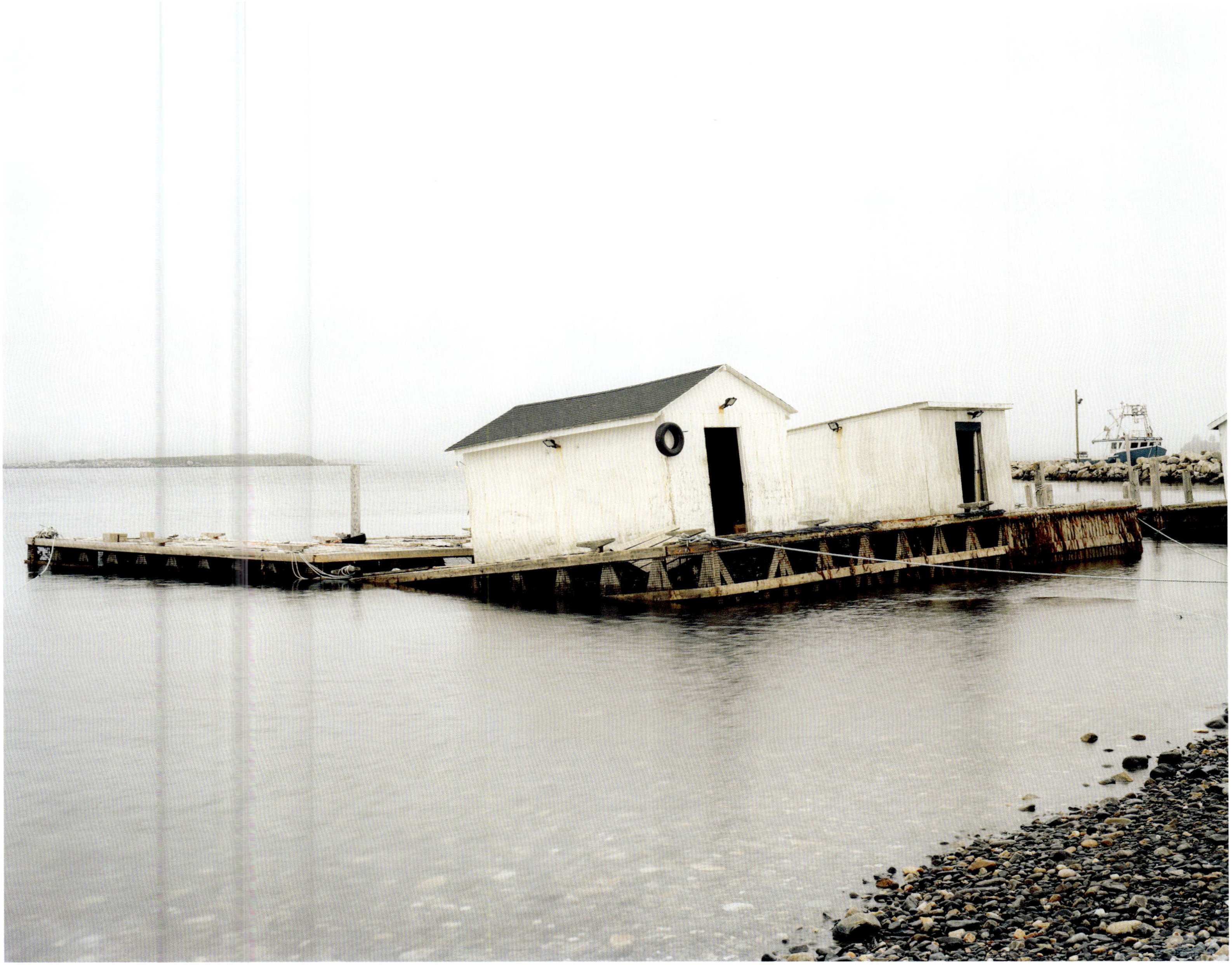

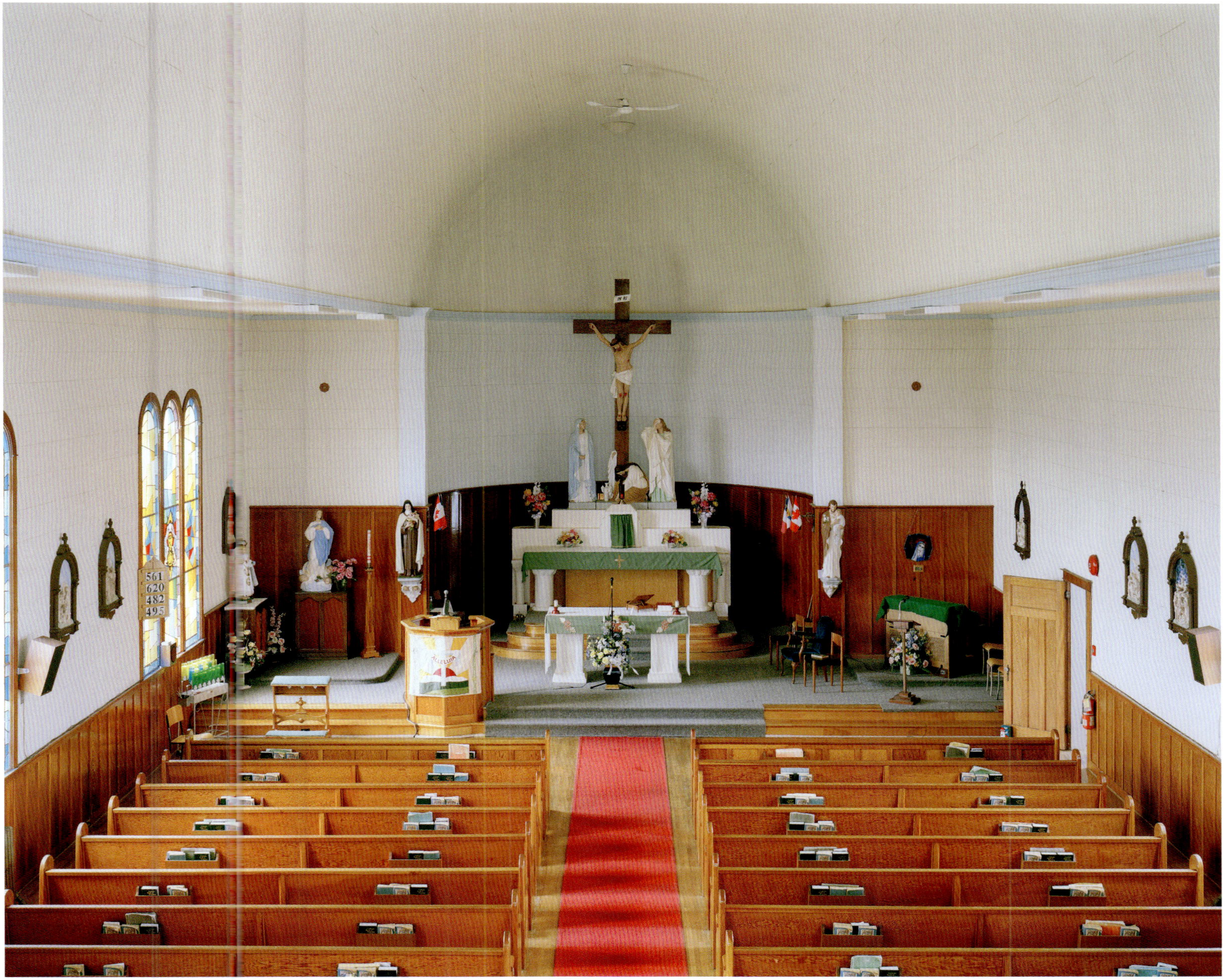
561
620
482
495

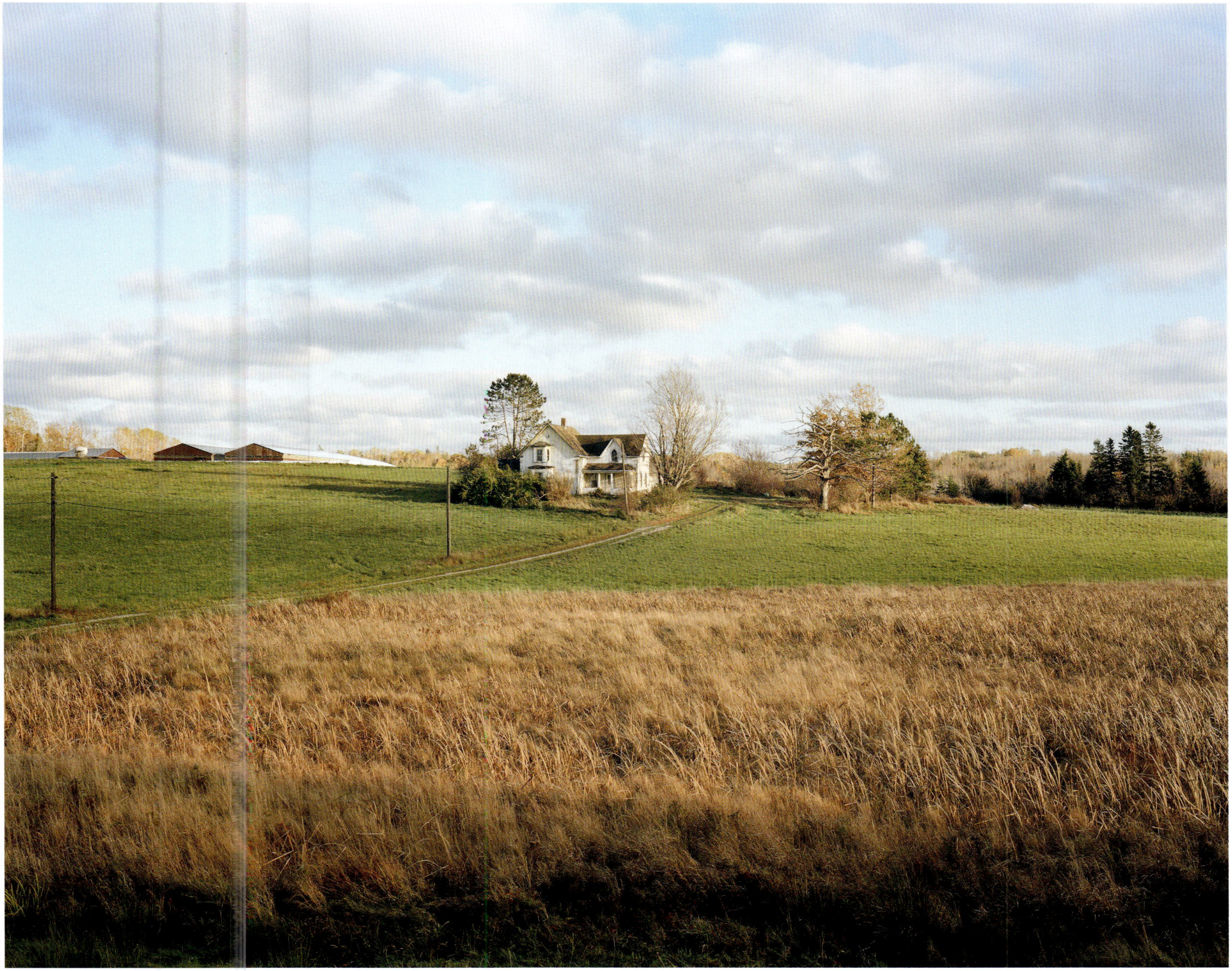

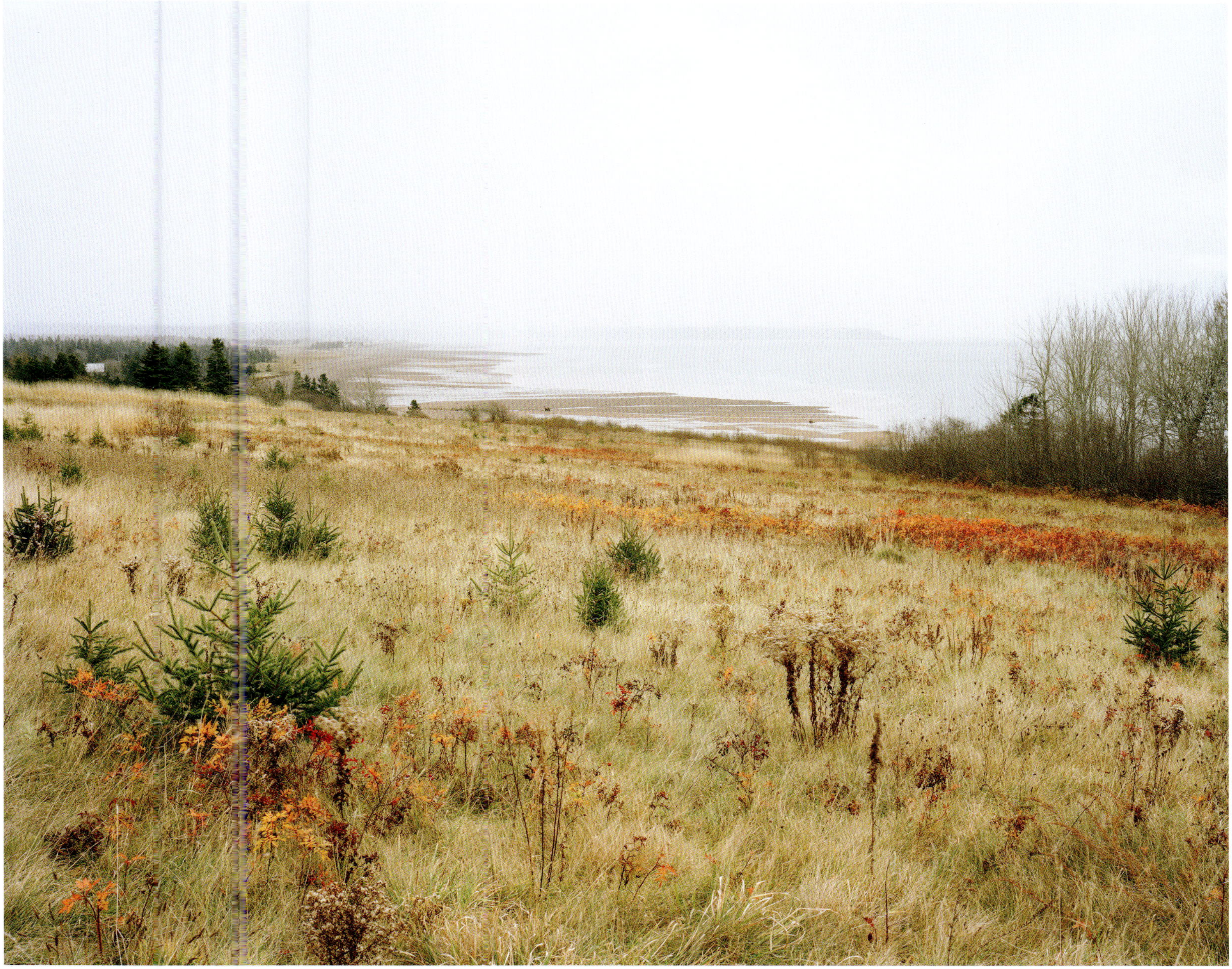

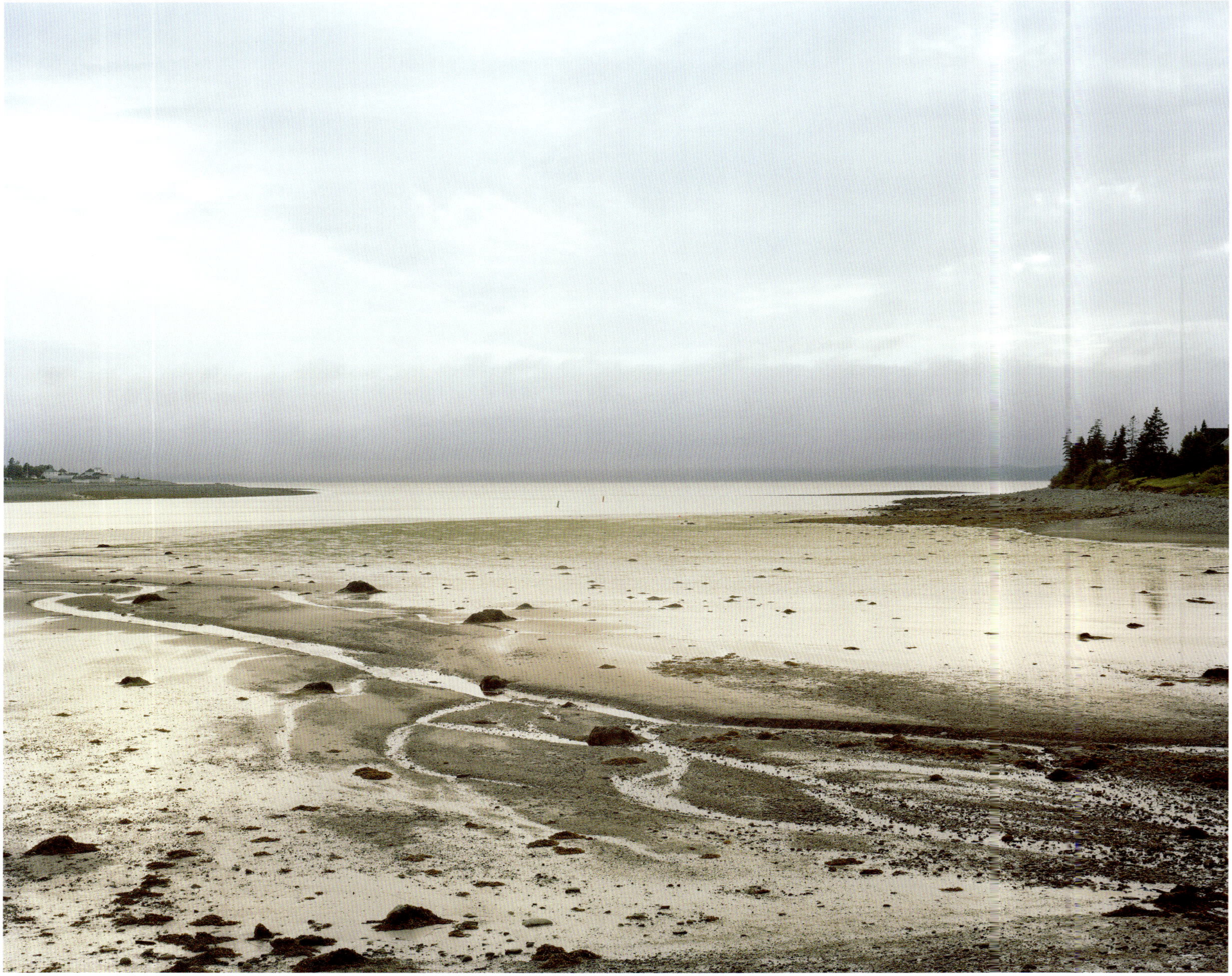

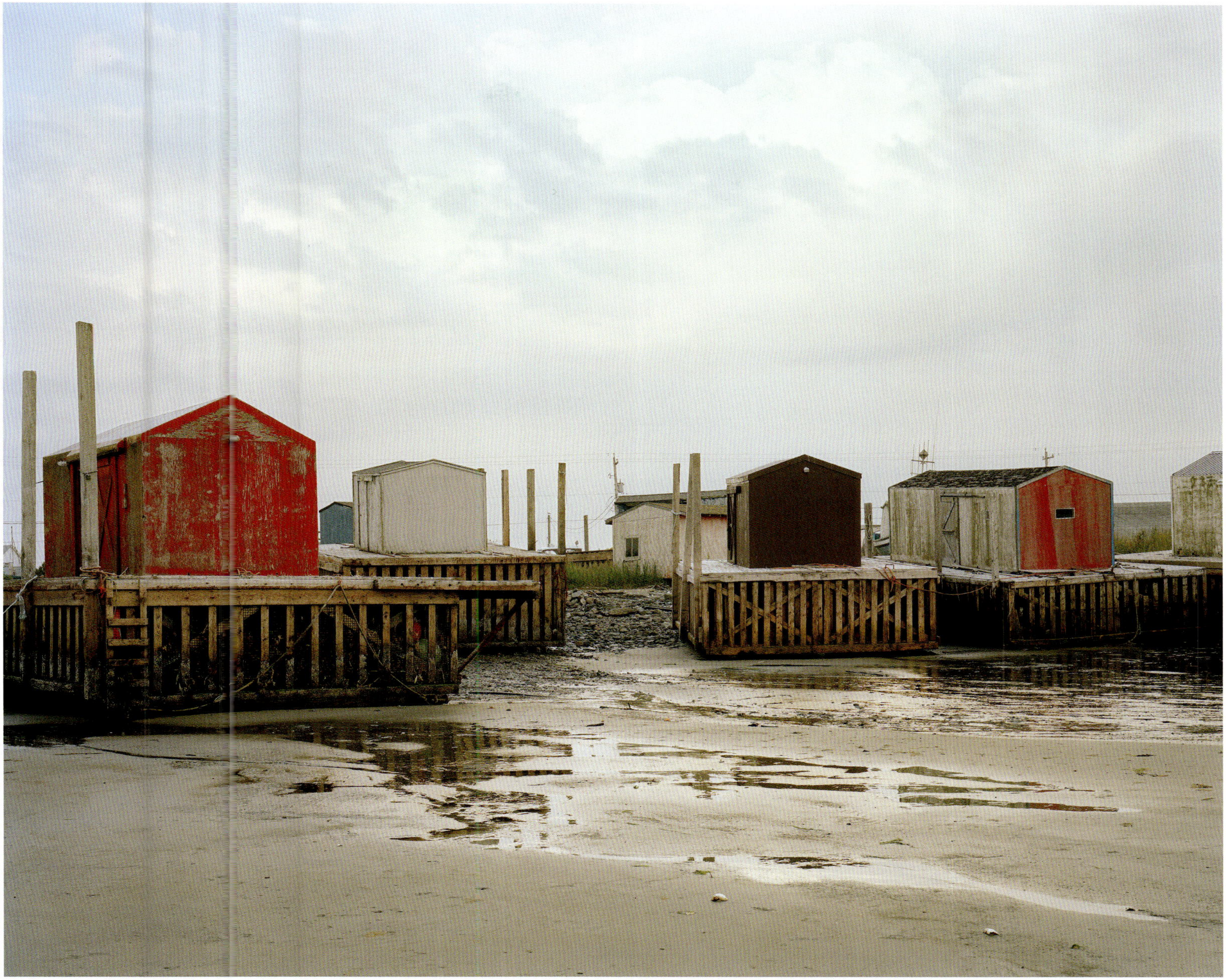

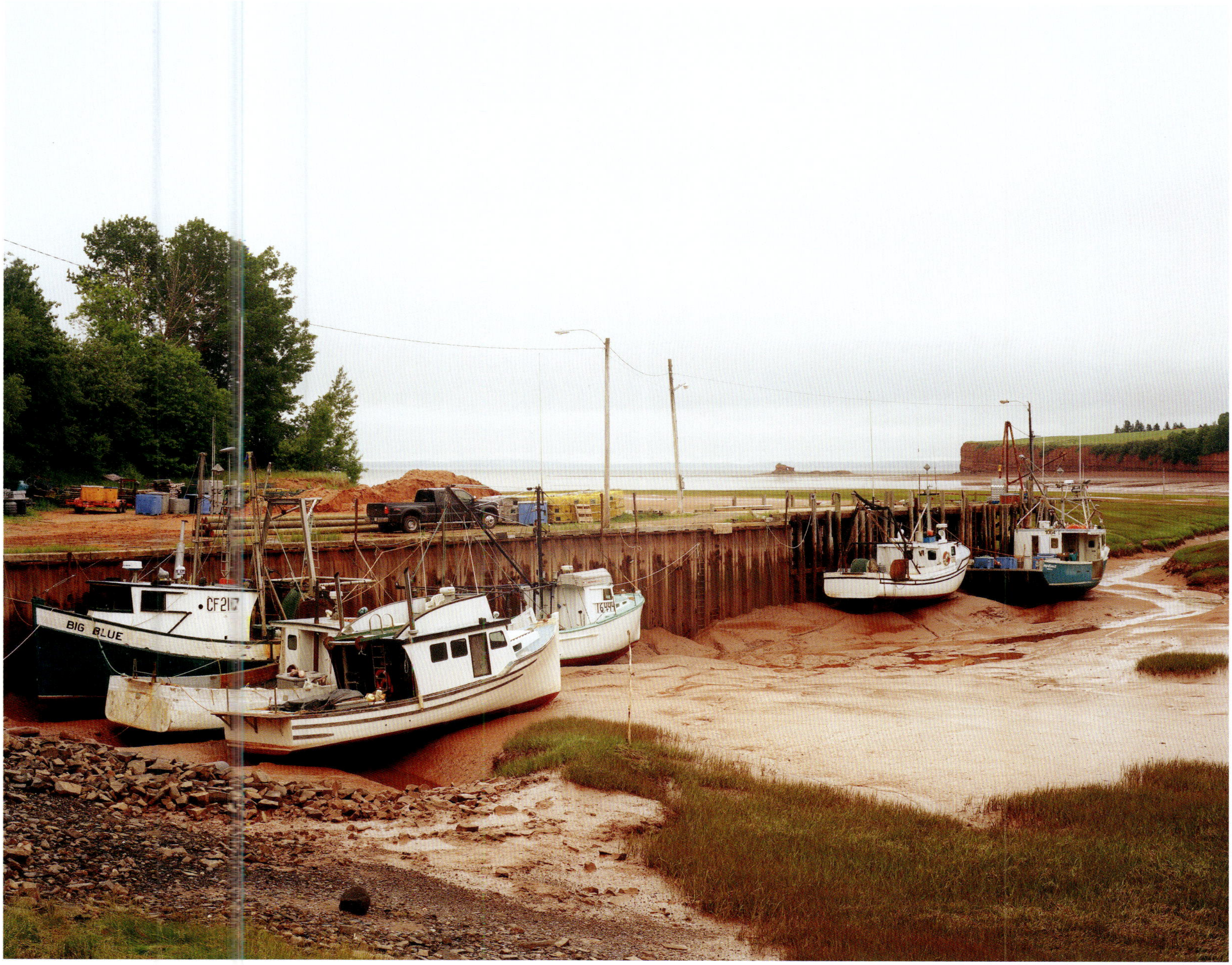
BIG BLUE

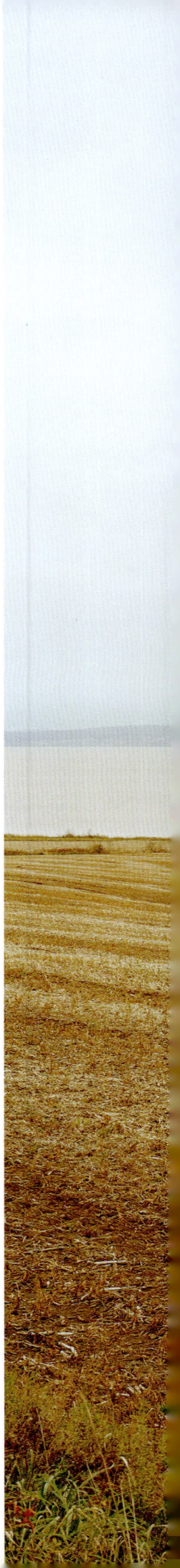

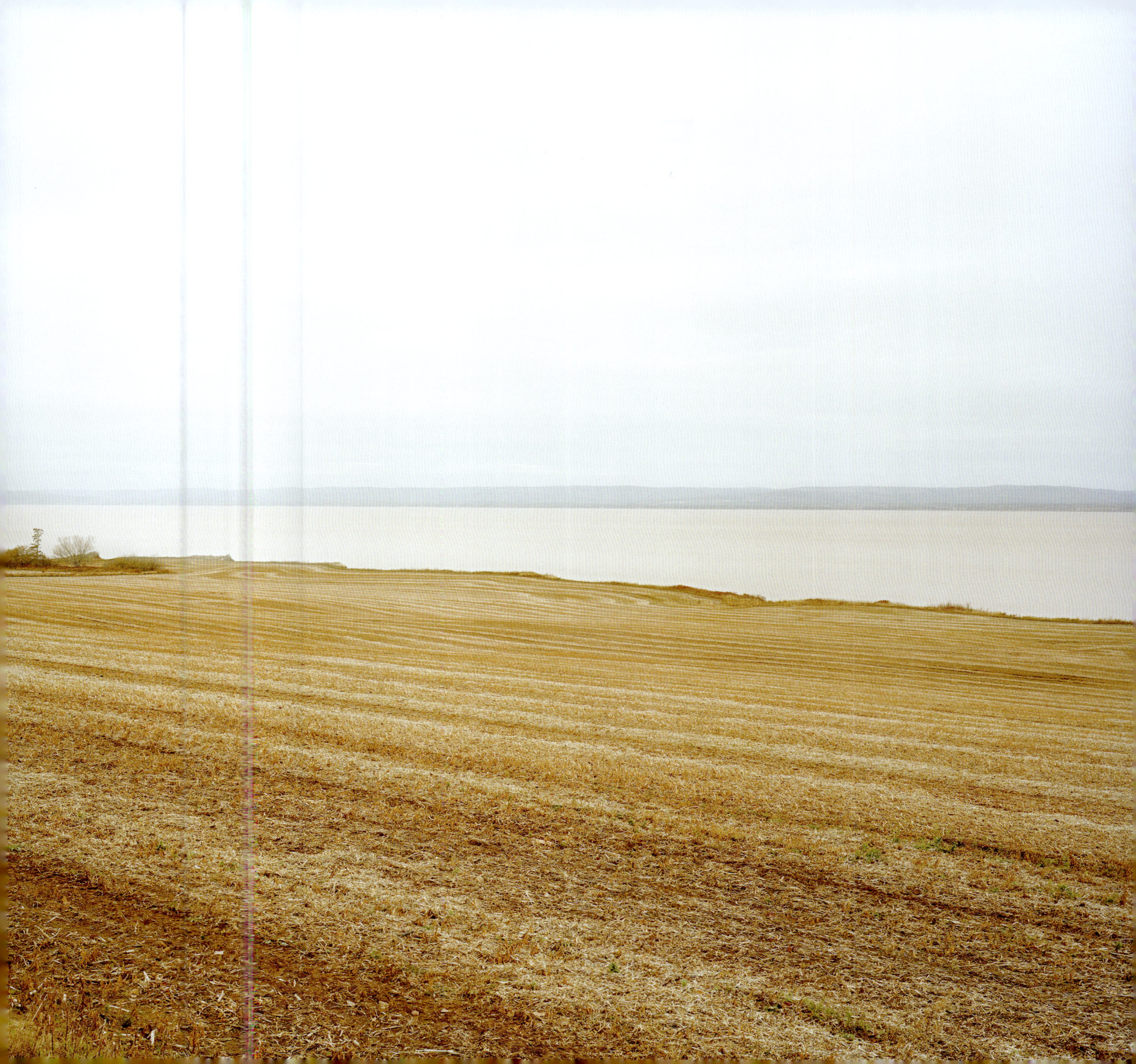

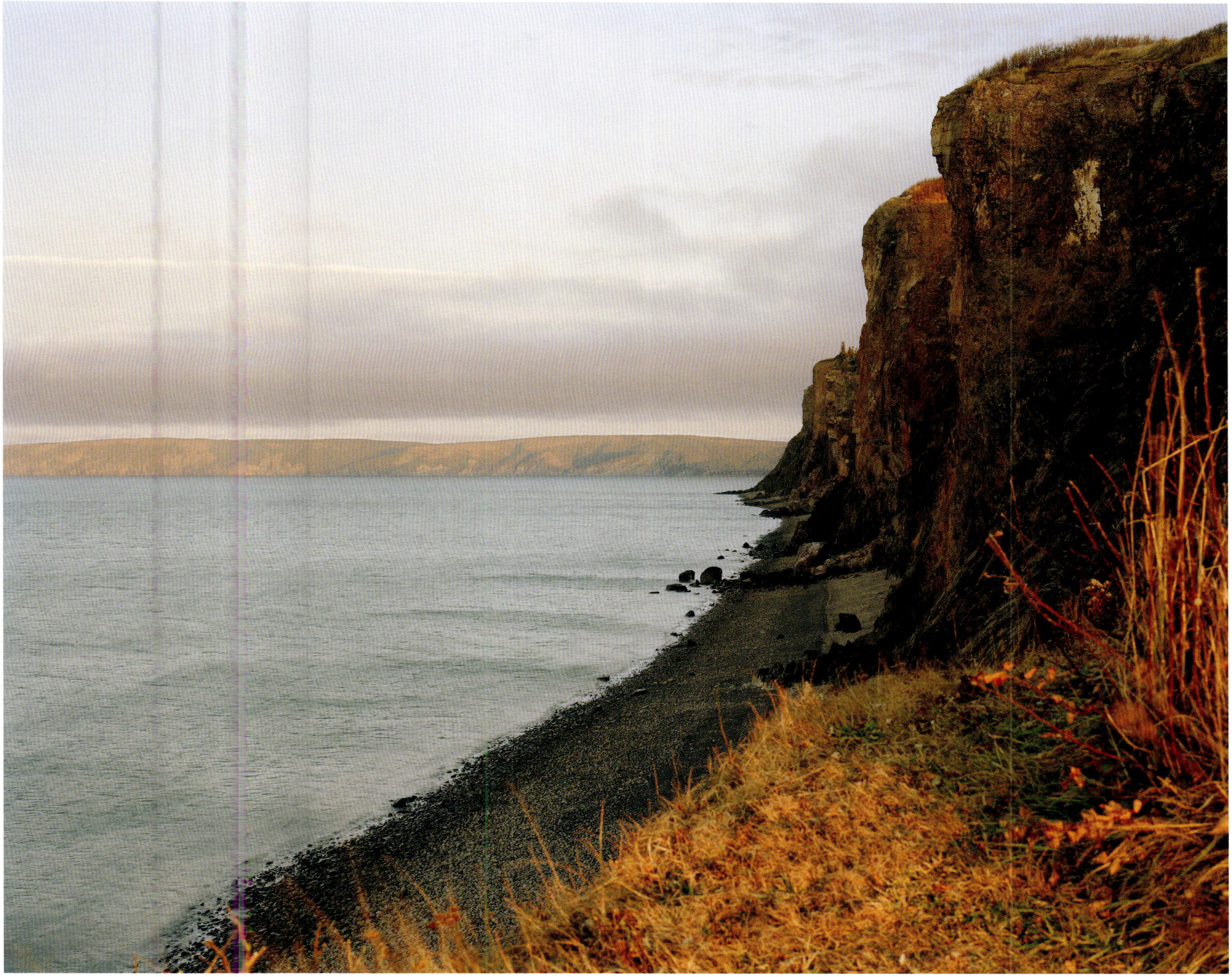

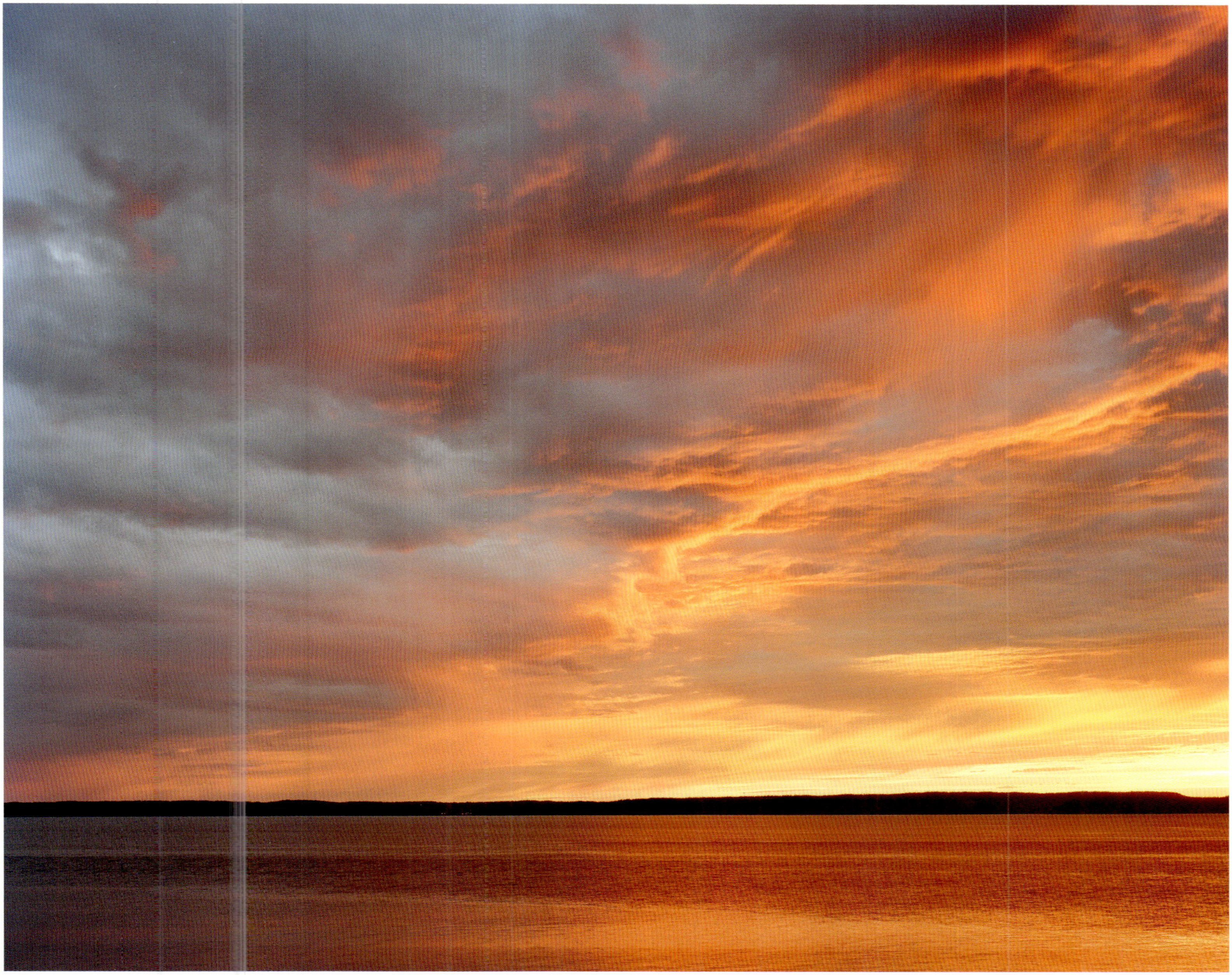

Still stands the forest primeval; but under the shade of its branches
Dwells another race, with other customs and language.
Only along the shore of the mournful and misty Atlantic
Linger a few Acadian peasants, whose fathers from exile
Wandered back to their native land to die in its bosom.
In the fisherman's cot the wheel and the loom are still busy;
Maidens still wear their Norman caps and their kirtles of homespun,
And by the evening fire repeat Evangeline's story,
While from its rocky caverns the deep-voiced, neighboring ocean
Speaks, and in accents disconsolate answers the wail of the forest.

— H. W. Longfellow, 1847

Afterword

Evangeline and I first met in a moment of serendipity. In early 2012 I was skimming Longfellow's collected works for passages to inspire a seemingly unrelated project about his birthplace and my adopted home, Portland, Maine. Only a few days earlier I had received notice of acceptance to an artist residency in Nova Scotia. My original intent was to photograph intertidal landscapes, but the approaching trip was about to take a much more ambitious direction.

Having no prior knowledge of *Evangeline* or the expulsion of the Acadians—the historical event upon which the poem is based—I stumbled upon the epic and was instantly captivated. I studied up on the deportation and read the poem repeatedly. I went to work photographing the Canadian province in June with Longfellow's words ringing in my ears. The mission to create a modern visual representation of the Acadia described by Longfellow in 1847 would draw me back to the region four times in as many years. The poet never visited Nova Scotia, but his vivid descriptions of the landscape could not have been more accurate. And the feelings of loss and desolation that the poem evokes still haunt the region today.

Nova Scotia is one of three provinces in eastern Canada known collectively as the Maritimes. It is a narrow peninsula almost entirely surrounded by the sea. Most of the images in this book were taken along the roadway dubbed the Evangeline Trail, the name being evidence of the importance of Longfellow's poem to the history of the province. This road traverses the western shore from Yarmouth in the south to the hallowed site of Grand-Pré on the shore of Minas Basin, a branch of the Bay of Fundy. Here, the largest tidal range in the world transforms the coastal landscape by exposing and recovering vast expanses of the sea floor twice daily. It feels as if the whole ocean is breathing in and out, in a semi-diurnal cadence. The rich valleys and lowlands are highly cultivated, while still feeling wild. Eagles hunt from coastal pine trees, seals lounge on sun-warmed rocks, and the wind can be unrelenting. Fog banks lurk around lush green headlands, creeping into coves and sweeping across the flats. Nestled into the scenery, a stoic culture, descended from Acadian settlers who were allowed to return from exile in the late 18th century, has adapted to living in harmony with the harsh elements. Life for the Acadians has never been easy. They have fought and toiled for everything they have. But as one travels through Nova Scotia today, the abundance of vacant properties and waning commerce in some areas suggest that forces beyond their control are once again putting a strain on the peaceful enclave.

Longfellow's *Evangeline* is based on a true story about loss and displacement. It is about a thriving village raised out of an inhospitable landscape by an industrious group of settlers, then eliminated in one abrupt event. Today along the Western Shore, a similar story is slowly unfolding. Many communities that were built with pride by a generation that banded together to reclaim their homeland a century ago are again declining in population as economic hardships stifle growth. The visual narrative I have weaved implies that these conditions have brought on a new migration of Acadians away from their homeland. It has been a gradual exodus compared with the Expulsion, but disturbing nonetheless. The decaying Victorian houses, deserted commercial fishing ports, and enchanting primordial landscapes—these are all verses in my own modern tale of Acadia.

— Mark Marchesi

Index

Thanks

to the following individuals and organizations who have supported this project, and my photographic works in general:

Maine College of Art & the Jenny Family

Patty & Cyrus Hagge

Eunice Panetta

Susan Lyons

Gary Astrachan

Bruce Brown

Maine Arts Commission

Christoph Irmscher